CONTENTS

KW-451-242

PREFACE

This resource has been written specifically to help candidates improve their chances of achieving a higher grade at GCSE Business Studies. It has been developed in such a way to allow teachers to use it with their students or, to allow students to work through the material independently. It was never our intention to provide a highly visual resource which is light on substance and does not allow access to higher grades. Candidates should be able to either 'dip into' the resource to improve understanding of certain topics, or work through the whole of it at the end of their course as they prepare for their examinations.

The resource has been designed to be used in conjunction with existing GCSE course books and the notes which students will have accumulated during their course. It is not intended to be a course book but a resource which provides '**triggers**', such as those found in the **Revision Activity**, to help remind students about what they have learned and how this information may be used in different contexts. The **Putting it into Context** section will provide an opportunity for students to see how their knowledge and understanding of a particular topic can be set within a particular context, similar to some of the scenarios used in examination papers.

We are aware that schools and candidates may be preparing for different specifications and options. However, as this resource is not intended to replace a basic textbook, but to support and help students for the final examination, we have deliberately not attempted to identify any of the information as being relevant to a particular specification or option.

The activities we have included have been designed to help reinforce learning and preparation for the final examination. In some cases, these activities will take a very different approach to those which students have probably experienced in class. In other cases, the activities may be very similar. The **Introduction** gives further information on preparation for the final examination.

The contents of this resource are also based on our collective experience as examiners and teachers of GCSE Business Studies. Detailed information is provided on the **question types** which candidates should expect to find in the examination papers dealing with the main specification content of GCSE Business Studies.

We have also tried to provide an insight into the high quality answers and the problems, mistakes and misunderstandings which candidates often make in examinations, by including **student answers** to examination type questions. Student responses to questions are based on answers written by students but selected and adapted to illustrate particular points. Higher Tier examination questions are targeted primarily at grades A* to B whilst common questions are targeted at grades C and D. We have deliberately avoided including a large number of knowledge recall type questions.

What the Examiner Says gives information on what the examiner may be looking for in answer to a question. It must be remembered that the questions are targeted at the **higher end of the ability range for GCSE**. We have done this deliberately, for the purpose of this book is to help candidates achieve higher grades and therefore there would be little point in not having high expectations of candidate answers. Candidate names do not refer to any one particular candidate but have been included to add an element of reality and improve readability.

In the **Case Study** section, we have provided a stimulus and some guidance on how students might use stimulus material to prepare for the examination. Students should be able to see from the information how questions can be developed from stimulus material. There is little point in having a pre-seen Case Study without doing some preparation by considering the types of questions which may be asked. The **Examination Questions** section is split into the main areas of study of a GCSE Business Studies course. Students will be able to choose Higher Tier type questions on a topic-by-topic basis. We have, though, included some Foundation Tier questions for extra practice.

Finally some thanks. Firstly to Colin Goodlad of Hodder Arnold in helping with the preparation of the material. Secondly to the many thousands of candidates whom we have both taught and examined over the years who have given us the ideas for this resource. We wish we could have been able to help you! Secondly to our families who have, once again, been very patient and understanding whilst we completed the task.

We hope you find the resource helps with your examination preparation. Good luck!

GCSE Business Studies

PASS PLUS

for OCR

+ Peter Kennerdell
+ Alan Williams
+ Mike Schofield

Hodder & Stoughton

A MEMBER OF THE HODDER HEADLINE GROUP

Orders: please contact Bookpoint Ltd, 130 Milton Park, Abingdon, Oxon OX14 4SB. Telephone: (44) 01235 827720. Fax: (44) 01235 400454. Lines are open from 9.00 – 6.00, Monday to Saturday, with a 24 hour message answering service. You can also order through our website www.hodderheadline.co.uk.

British Library Cataloguing in Publication Data
A catalogue record for this title is available from the British Library

ISBN 0 340 87302 7

First Published 2003
Impression number   10 9 8 7 6 5 4 3 2 1
Year   2007 2006 2005 2004 2003

Copyright © 2003 Peter Kennerdell, Mike Schofield and Alan Williams

Typeset by Pantek Arts Ltd.
Printed in Spain for Hodder & Stoughton Educational, a division of Hodder Headline Plc, 338 Euston Road, London, NW1 3BH.

PART ONE

INTRODUCTION – PREPARING FOR THE EXAMINATION

This chapter of the book is to help you to prepare for the examination(s) that you will sit in Business Studies.

No advice is given about coursework in this book. You will find plenty of advice about coursework in textbooks or provided by the examination board. The book, *Business Studies for OCR GCSE*, published by Hodder and Stoughton, has a separate section (Section 8) which provides detailed guidance. OCR also provides a Coursework Guidance Pack. This gives samples of coursework and comments about what is good and bad in each piece of work.

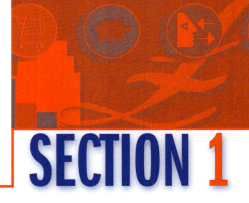

The Examination

SECTION 1

It is the job of an examiner who writes a GCSE paper to set questions that give the candidate the opportunity to show what they know, understand and can do. The examiner is not trying to set trick questions! You can be confident that if you have prepared yourself properly, you will get the result that you deserve.

Preparation will lead to success

OCR Business Studies examinations involve a number of questions that will be set around one or more real or imaginary business situations. Most of the questions will be based around these business situations.

Most GCSE Business Studies examinations are designed to test four skills known as 'Assessment Objectives'. (The exception is the Case Study Paper which can be taken instead of presenting coursework.) These assessment objectives can be summarised under the headings **knowledge**, **application**, **analysis** and **evaluation**. Words in the questions, called **command words**, will help you to know what skill is being tested. It is worth knowing a little about assessment objectives and command words – it will help you to write high scoring answers. The assessment objectives are explained in the boxes below:

Knowledge This is about the meaning of terms and ideas. Typical command words that indicate knowledge questions are *list*, *state* and *explain*. For example:

- State the 4Ps connected with marketing.
- Explain the meaning of the term marketing.

With 'knowledge' questions you do **not** need to write about the business situations given in the examination paper.

Application This skill is about using knowledge or skills to discuss or calculate something about the business in the examination paper. *Explain* is a typical command word – but in this type of question you will be asked to explain how something affects the business in the examination paper. Calculate is another common command word telling you to apply your numeracy skills. Example questions are:

- Explain how John Taylor, as a sole trader, will be affected by unlimited liability.
- Calculate the percentage mark-up on goods bought in at 15p and sold at 25p.

Analysis This is about using information to discuss or break down a problem – most commonly in Business Studies you need to discuss the advantages and disadvantages of something. You may also be required to interpret data, for example, comparing trends and making predictions (often some form of calculation may be involved). Typical commands in a question may be *compare* or *discuss* or a longer statement such as *explain the advantages and disadvantages* of something. Example questions are:

- Discuss the changes that may have caused the rise in turnover between 1998 and 1999.
- State and explain the benefits and problems that the local council should take into consideration when deciding whether or not to approve planning application for a new airport.

Evaluation This is about making judgements. You may need to decide how well a business has performed or suggest what a business should do. Your judgement will be based on either evidence (data in the question or your own knowledge) or reasoned argument – often a discussion of pros and cons of a course of action. Typical command words are *evaluate* and *recommend*. Example questions are:

- Using the information in the Trading and Profit and Loss Account (and/or Balance Sheet), evaluate the performance of the business in 2002 compared with 2001.
- Recommend whether or not John Taylor should go into partnership or remain as a sole trader.

MULTI-SKILL QUESTIONS

In practice, to answer most questions successfully, you need to use more than one of the four skills. Evaluation questions usually need you to apply your knowledge to give an analysis of a problem before making a judgement.

MARK SCHEMES

Questions may be marked using either a 'points' system or 'levels of response' mark scheme. In a points system, one mark is usually given for each correct statement – each correct item in a list or correct statement in an explanation of a term. Levels of response mark schemes are often used for longer questions, with a high mark allocation, that require analysis and evaluation. The following question and mark scheme illustrate this.

Question Jason Lee is leaving Colliers PLC (a chocolate manufacturer and retailer) and intends to open a shop selling chocolates and sweets. Should he open a shop as a franchise or as an independent shop? Discuss the advantages and disadvantages of each option to give reasons for your answer.

Mark Scheme

Level One • The candidate discusses the advantages of one option – either opening as a franchise or as an independent trader.

Level Two • The candidate discusses the advantages/disadvantages of both options.

Level Three • The candidate comes to a conclusion and gives a reason for the decision.

WRITING FRAMES

A neat way to make sure that you write good answers to analysis and evaluation questions is to use writing frames like the one below.

Advantages/Strengths/ Arguments for	Disadvantages/Weaknesses/ Arguments against

Reasons for conclusion/decision/recommendation

For example, a writing frame for the question marked using a levels of response mark scheme given above would be:

Arguments for opening as a franchise	Arguments against opening as a franchise
• Tried and tested product • Support/advice from franchiser • Advertising undertaken by franchiser	• Royalty must be paid to franchiser • Owner does not have total control • Must buy stock from franchiser

Reasons for conclusion/decision/recommendation

Open as an independent – Jason has worked in chocolate business so has knowledge/skills necessary to succeed.

OR

Open as a franchise – more chance of success, the majority of small, independent businesses do not last more than 12 months.

SO WHAT? OR CONSEQUENCE DIAGRAMS

These are another useful way to get your ideas together to answer a question. Businesses are affected by all kinds of changes. A 'So What?' or 'Consequence' diagram shows the sequence of changes that may take place after something is altered. The following is an example of a question that asks you to say what will happen to the business as a result of a change:

Question Explain how a rise in interest rates will affect XYZ Ltd

CONSEQUENCE DIAGRAM:

Interest rates rise ⟶ cost of borrowing rises ⟶ XYZ may consider raising prices to cover rise in costs ⟶ sales may fall due to price rise ⟶ profits may fall ⟶ redundancies may follow ⟶ the business may close.

In this example, the business may be affected in another way – a second Consequence Diagram is needed.

Interest rates rise ⟶ consumers have less disposable income ⟶ demand falls (for certain goods) ⟶ sales fall due to fall in demand ⟶ and so on down to the business folding.

These consequence diagrams help you to learn to explain fully sequences of events. This can help you to score high marks – whether a points or levels of response mark scheme is used.

Revising for the Examination

SECTION 2

There will be a lot to revise for a Business Studies GCSE examination. This section explains some useful techniques for revision and gives some advice about planning a revision programme.

BEFORE YOU START

Make sure that the room you use is organised. You should work at a desk and in good light – natural or electric. Have paper, pens, rulers, rubbers and so on to hand. If you want to listen to music do so – but you should not listen to a radio programme with a DJ who may become a distraction. The best music to listen to is instrumental music – perhaps this is the time to get into classical music! Have regular breaks when you walk around, have a drink or something to eat. Do not make these breaks too frequent – you should be able to work for at least 30 minutes without one.

TECHNIQUES OF REVISION

Very few people are able to read something and then remember it in detail. Revising is hard work. It is best done by being active – by writing or drawing or creating something. There is no single way to revise. We all have different styles of learning – some like to make notes, others like images such as pictures and diagrams, others like to be physically active. You should choose revision techniques that suit your learning style. Different parts of Business Studies suit different revision techniques. You should also use different techniques so that there is some variety in your work. The following are some useful revision techniques.

KNOWLEDGE HIERARCHIES OR SUMMARY LISTS

Long sets of notes can be difficult to learn. Summarising them into a list of key words is fantastically helpful. Columns are used to organise the words into a 'hierarchy' – the most important terms go to the left of the page in the first column, lesser terms in the next columns.

As well as the example that follows, there are further examples throughout this book. Note that a knowledge hierarchy is different from brainstorming – with hierarchies the information is organised and classified into groups. They need to be neat – it helps to create a 'picture' that you will remember in the exam.

The following summarises the important terms related to the 4Ps of marketing.

The Marketing Mix

Topic	Key Features	Detail	Further Information
Product	• Customer wants • Product range/mix	• Design • Features • Job	• Size, colour
Price	• Competition-based • Penetration price • Creaming/Skimming • Cost plus pricing	• Higher • Lower • Same • Low then raise price • High then lower price • Add profit margin	• Exclusive • Switch customer to you • Distinguish by using a different form of competition • Gain market share • Make profit, then increase sales • Depends on what customers will pay
Place	• Direct to customer or • Through wholesaler/retailer	• Vending machine • Mail order • Internet • Farmer's roadside stall • Shop	
Promotion	• Advertising • Sales Promotions	• Direct or • Indirect • Persuasive or • Informative • Buy one get one free • Added value • Price reductions • Loss leaders • Competitions • Free samples • Merchandising • After-sales service	• To specific individuals • To anyone watching • Often plays on emotions • Gives factual details

You will find another, slightly different version of this list in the unit about Marketing. There is no 'right' or 'wrong' list. **The list that you will remember is the one that you draw up yourself**. You are strongly advised to try to create your own and, then, perhaps compare it with the one in the book. You will remember much more from creating your own than from reading an example. To create one you should go through the notes that your teacher has given to you or through a chapter in a textbook.

You will find that creating the list helps you to remember. The next time you revise marketing you may only need to learn the first two columns – they will 'trigger off' all the other points. When you know it well enough, you will only need to remember the first four words – product, price, place and promotion – and these will remind you of everything else.

MIND MAPS OR STAR DIAGRAMS

These do a similar job to summary lists. Some people, particularly those who like visual things (diagrams, pictures), find mind maps more useful than lists. The following mind map summarises some key points about introducing technology into production in manufacturing industry. Like knowledge hierarchies, the information in a mind map should be organised logically.

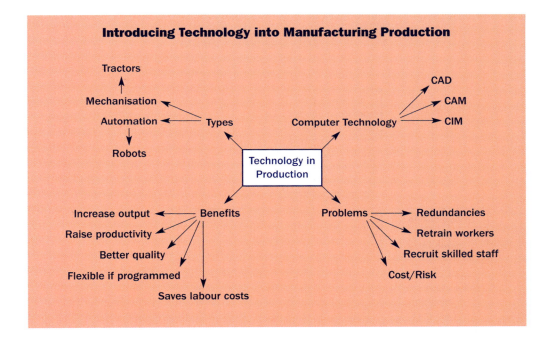

Introducing Technology into Manufacturing Production

Tractors
Mechanisation
Automation ← Types
Robots

CAD
CAM
Computer Technology → CIM

Technology in Production

Increase output ← Benefits
Raise productivity
Better quality
Flexible if programmed
Saves labour costs

Problems → Redundancies
Retrain workers
Recruit skilled staff
Cost/Risk

FLOW CHARTS

These are useful for summarising a chain or sequence of events that might happen. The following may help to revise the difference between unlimited and limited liability.

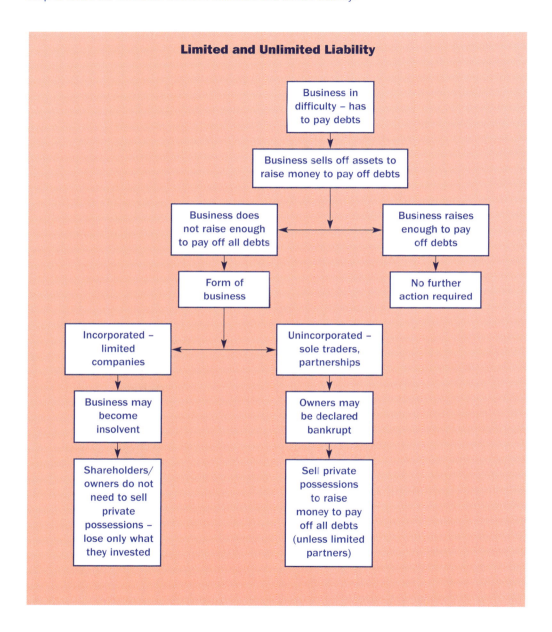

GCSE Business Studies Pass Plus for OCR

IMAGE CHAINS

Like flow charts, these are useful for learning sequences of events. Instead of boxes with words in them, they use boxes with pictures or cartoons. The following image chain shows the sequence of events for recruiting and selecting a new worker.

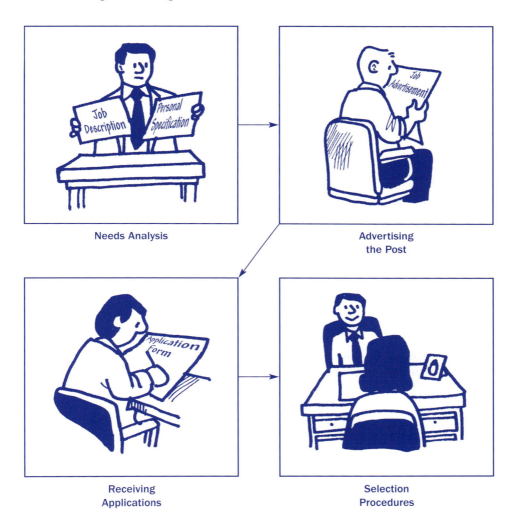

Needs Analysis

Advertising
the Post

Receiving
Applications

Selection
Procedures

PICTURES

Labelling a picture with key words is another technique. The following is a reminder of what a person specification is and the sources of information the employer can use to tell if the person meets the specification.

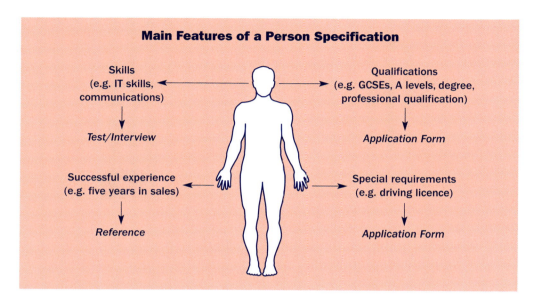

WORD ASSOCIATIONS

An alternative to a diagram is word association. Link a key term with another term to help you to remember. For example, to help to remember the points about person specifications, you might link the key words as follows:

- My big brain = qualifications
- The teacher's grey hair = experience
- Hands = skills
- My big nose = special requirements.

POEMS, RAPS AND (SILLY) STORIES

Students who are creative or are musical often like poems, raps or silly stories. They are good for learning a list of terms. The poem, rap or story should include all the terms that you need to learn. These do not need to be very good – it is writing them that is useful. The sillier they are the more you will remember them. The following poem (it mostly rhymes!) revises the meaning and the different types of economies of scale.

Ode to Economies of Scale

When *Average* costs fall
The big boss has a ball
Economies of scale cut the cost
To competition, sales are not lost
Economies can be *financial*
Or may be *managerial*
Some, called *risk-bearing*,
Sort of rhyme with *marketing*
Technical economies are about how to make
But all this poetry is giving me a headache.

Planning Revision

SECTION 3

PLANNING YOUR REVISION

The average person needs to revise things three or four times. When we learn something for the first time, we will forget 80% of it within 24 hours. Each time you revise, more of what you learn stays firmly in the memory.

You will find it useful to make a plan. This will help you to organise yourself so that you get things done and make progress. Follow the steps suggested below. You might do this planning once every month in the period leading up to the examination.

Step One: Self-Review

This will help you to think about what you need to concentrate on in order to improve your work. You write down what you are confident about in your studies and those things that you think are your main weaknesses. Use the self-review sheet on page 14. Alternatively, your teacher may have given you lists of things to know about each topic in Business Studies. Tick and cross items on the list depending on how well you feel you know them. If not, your teacher can get lists from OCR (they are in the published schemes of work). It will boost your confidence each time you review a topic – you should have become confident about more things.

Step Two: Study Timetable

This is your weekly plan. This is really important for helping you 'to make things happen'. You need to write down exactly what you will do each day for your revision – you should write SMART targets (see Setting Revision Targets on page 15). You could use the weekly planner on page 16.

Step Three: Make it Happen

Carry out your weekly plan. You will find it useful to write down any work that you find difficult – seek help perhaps from your teacher to overcome the problem.

Step Five: Self-Review

At the end of the month, complete another self-review. Write more plans for the next month's work.

SELF-REVIEW: STRENGTHS AND WEAKNESSES

The purpose of this sheet to help you to think about what topics you need to work on to improve. In the 'Strengths' column, for each topic, write down three things that you think you have done or know well. In the 'Weaknesses' column, write down three things you need to improve.

Topic	Strengths	Weaknesses
External environment of business	1 2 3	1 2 3
Business structure and organisation	1 2 3	1 2 3
Marketing	1 2 3	1 2 3
Production	1 2 3	1 2 3
Finance	1 2 3	1 2 3
People in organisations	1 2 3	1 2 3
Aiding and controlling business activity	1 2 3	1 2 3
Option (Marketing or Business and change)	1 2 3	1 2 3

SETTING REVISION TARGETS

Targets that you set should be SMART.

Use these questions to check that you write SMART targets.

Specific
Do my targets say exactly what I need to do?

Measureable
How will I be able to prove that I have met my targets?

Achievable
Will I be able to achieve my target in the time?

Realistic
Are my targets about action that I can take?

Time-related
Have I set deadlines for meeting my targets?

SMART targets are:

Specific

Measureable

Achievable

Realistic

Time-related

Revision Targets – are these targets SMART?

Which of these targets do you think are SMART?

- I will revise my Business Studies.
- I will make notes on economies of scale.
- I will learn 20 terms connected with the Marketing by Thursday.
- Tonight I will write a revision action plan for next week.
- I will read notes on Production Techniques.
- I will write a rap about ratios used to analyse balance sheets tonight.

STUDY TIMETABLE

For the week beginning _____ Name _____

Times	Monday	Tuesday	Wednesday	Thursday	Friday	Times	Saturday	Sunday
Morning	School	School	School	School	School	9 – 10		
Afternoon	School	School	School	School	School	10 – 11		
4.15 – 5.00						11 – 12		
5.00 – 5.30						12 – 1		
5.30 – 6.30						1 – 2		
6.30 – 7.00						3 – 4		
7.00 – 7.30						4 – 6		
7.30 – 8.00						6 – 7		
8.00 – 8.30						7 – 8		
8.30 – 9.00						8 – 9		

In the Examination

If you have revised thoroughly, you can be confident about sitting the examination. Remember, it is the job of the examiner who writes the paper to set a paper that tests what you know, understand and can do – not to try to catch you out with trick questions. The following rules may help you to do justice to your ability.

- Make sure that you go into the examination with all the equipment that you need – pens, pencils, rulers, rubbers and a calculator.
- At the beginning of the examination take your time – do not panic and rush your work.
- Read the questions carefully. Make sure that you understand what the question is asking you to do.
- Obey any specific instructions such as 'Show your working' or 'State and explain TWO...'.
- Develop fully the points you wish to make.
- Use the specialist Business Studies terms that you have learnt.
- Remember that writing frames can help for longer, analysis and evaluation questions.
- Write neatly.
- Take care when drawing diagrams – be sure to label them.
- Write clearly – remember that some questions have additional marks for the Quality of Written Communications.
- Answer ALL the questions as instructed.

Using this Book

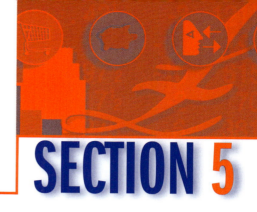

SECTION 5

In Part Two of the book, each section deals with a specific part of the OCR GCSE Business Studies Specification. Each section is divided into the following sub-sections.

SOME BASICS

This is intended to remind you briefly of the main areas of the topic – very little detail is given here. The aim is to see how the different areas fit together within the topic.

Revision Material

KNOWLEDGE HIERARCHIES OR SUMMARY LISTS

These provide you with main terms that are connected with the topic. Working to the right, each column provides additional detail. Learning these is very useful. Better still, use your notes and your Business Studies textbook to create your own knowledge hierarchy – it is not easy but you can be sure you will remember more from doing this compared with reading the one in the book. Compare the one you make with the one in the book.

PUTTING IT IN CONTEXT

This sub-section shows how the main ideas can be applied to business situations to explain, analyse or evaluate them. For candidates who want to perform at the highest level, knowing how to apply your knowledge in this way is vital. You are recommended to read over the section before attempting any relevant question(s).

ACTIVITIES

These are short activities that you may find useful to check your understanding before dealing with longer, examination type questions. Additionally or instead, you might want to use some of the revision techniques suggested earlier in this Introduction to make absolutely sure that you are completely familiar with the topic.

You will find a list of question types connected with the content of the section varying from (usually straightforward) knowledge type questions to the more difficult analysis and evaluation question types.

Specimen Questions

In this sub-section you will find a range of higher (A–B) and common (C–D) questions covering the topic. You will also find an answer that has been written by a student and some comments by an examiner about this answer. The answers are not all perfect. It can be useful to read perfect answers. Equally, it can be useful to read answers that are not so good and then read the examiner's explanation about how the answer could have been improved – learning from mistakes is one of the best ways of learning.

One of the main failings of many candidates in examinations is that they do not use their knowledge fully to answer the questions that are set. Making use of the Specimen Questions should help you to avoid this. Above all you are recommended to use one or more of the following approaches to the Specimen Questions.

- Write an answer to the questions and then compare your answer with the student's answer and the comments from the examiner.
- Write notes, perhaps using a writing frame or consequence diagram, instead of a full written answer and then compare what you have written with the student's answer and the examiner's comments.
- Read the student's answer to a question and then try to write a better answer, using the advice from the examiner.

2

PART TWO

REVISING BUSINESS STUDIES

The Knowledge Hierarchies and the Activities in each of the units of this section should help students to recall the knowledge content of Business Studies. Primarily, though, this section is about the application of knowledge to analyse and evaluate business contexts. This is demonstrated in the Putting it in Context sections while the Questions Types to Expect, Student Answers and What the Examiner Says are designed to show how knowledge may be applied in the examination situation.

The External Environment of Business

SECTION 1

SOME BASICS

Organisations produce goods and services. Some are privately owned businesses and exist in the private sector of the economy, others are organisations owned by the state or government and exist in the public sector. They use resources (land, labour, capital and enterprise or organisation). Consumer goods satisfy consumer wants, capital goods are sold to businesses and public organisations to help them to produce more goods and services. Organisations usually set objectives, though these will differ depending on whether they are private or publicly owned.

All organisations can be classified as primary, secondary or tertiary sector organisations, depending on what they make. The relative importance of the three sectors has changed significantly in the past 100 years.

Stakeholders are people and organisations who are affected by business activity. Some will be affected by the private costs and benefits of the activity, others by the social costs and benefits.

Revision Material

KNOWLEDGE HIERARCHY: LIST OF THINGS TO KNOW ABOUT THE EXTERNAL ENVIRONMENT OF BUSINESS

This information is intended to provide a quick reminder. Your notes, and the information in the textbook you have used, should provide more detailed information and examples.

Topic	Key Features	Detail	Further Information
Economic problem	• Scarcity	• Unlimited wants	• Basic needs • Luxuries
		• Limited resources (factors of production)	• Land • Labour • Capital • Enterprise
	• Choice	• Who, What, Where, How to produce	
	• Opportunity cost	• Sacrifice connected with choice	• Mars or Yorkie bar

Topic	Key Features	Detail	Further Information
Goods and Services	• Consumer goods and services	• Clothing • Food • Houses • Entertainments • Holidays	
	• Capital goods	• Machines • Tools • Offices • Factories	
Sectors of the Economy (1)	• Primary	• Take raw materials from	• Farming • Fishing • Mining • Forestry
	• Secondary	• Manufacturing and construction industry	• Clothing • Building • Processed foods • Electrical goods
	• Tertiary	• Services	• Retailing • Leisure • Financial • Transport • Health
Objectives	• Survival • Profit • Provision of a service • Growth	• Sales • Market Share	
Sectors of the Economy (2)	• Private sector	• Privately owned businesses	• Sole traders • Partnerships • Limited companies • Co-operatives
	• Public organisations	• State/government owned organisations	• Health Service • BBC • Local councils • Police Force • Armed Forces
Stakeholders	• Workers and managers	• Jobs • Income	
	• Owners	• Profits • Capital appreciation	

Topic	Key Features	Detail	Further Information
Stakeholders *cont.*	• Customers	• Goods and services	
	• Suppliers	• Sales	
	• Competitors	• Sales	
	• Government	• Government spending • Taxation	• Social Security • Income tax • VAT
Benefits	• Private	• Income	• Profits • Wages, salaries
	• Social	• Jobs in the community • Spending in the community • Service for community	
Costs	• Private	• Fixed costs	• Rent for factory; shop
		• Variable costs	• Wages • Raw materials • Power
	• Social	• Pollution • Loss of land	• Air, noise, river • Scenery • Leisure facility • Natural habitats
Government	• Local	• Planning permission • Control pollution	
	• National	• Give grants • Laws and regulations	
Pressure Groups	• Business groups	• CBI • Trade Associations	
	• Consumer groups	• Consumer's Association	
	• Environmental groups	• Greenpeace • Friends of the Earth	
	• Worker groups	• Trade Unions • Professional Associations	

Examples of businesses in the primary sector

PUTTING IT IN CONTEXT

The economy of Moorshire has changed significantly in the past 20 years. Despite increases in the amount produced, employment in both the *primary* and *secondary* sectors continued to fall, with the greatest falls in the secondary sector. The fall is largely due to the increased use of *technology*, especially *computer integrated manufacturing* in secondary industries such as car assembly, chemical production and furniture manufacture. Output might have grown even more in both sectors but for the increase in the amount of raw materials and food and of manufactured goods that are now imported in the UK. Had this happened, employment levels in the primary and secondary sectors might not have fallen.

The *tertiary* sector has experienced rapid growth, both in output and employment. As the income of people in the county has risen, they have more money to spend in shops and on services such as leisure, recreation and tourism. The financial services such as banking, insurance and the savings industries have also grown rapidly. Many people, previously employed in the primary and secondary sectors, have found employment in the tertiary sector, though some too old or too set in their ways have not been prepared to undertake the necessary training to develop the new skills

Example of a business in the secondary sector

Examples of businesses in the tertiary sector

needed in the new economy. Overall employment has risen, though more jobs are part-time and workers are expected to be more flexible in the hours they work.

With the closure of the coal mining industry, the Moorshire County Council decided to build an industrial estate to attract new businesses to the area. The industrial estate has been a success, with owners generally reporting good profits. Some other *stakeholders* have been pleased by the *social benefits* that have resulted – the workers who built the new factories, people who work in the new factories, other businesses in Moorshire whose trade has increased because workers generally now have more money to spend and those businesses who supply materials and services to the new firms on the estates. Yet other stakeholders have been concerned about the *social costs* of the developments. Some have objected to the increase in traffic and the air and noise pollution that followed, whilst environmental groups, including the pressure group, Friends of the Earth, have been concerned about the loss of land the natural habitats of some wild animals.

The *objective* of the County Council in providing the industrial estate has been to provide a *service* to the community so that the people who live in it have jobs. The development has also increased the tax income of the Council which has meant that it is able to provide more or better services such as education and social services. Peter Winstanley started a small picture-framing business on the estate. His objective was to develop some regular customers and to make enough profit just to *survive* the first year in business. Catherine Tresor moved her car radio business to new premises on the industrial estate because, after three successful years, she believed she could *expand* the business to include auto electric services. She needed larger premises as well as new employees.

Pressure groups affect business

ACTIVITIES

ACTIVITY ONE

Use the words in the 'Words to use' list to complete the following diagram to explain the basic economic problem.

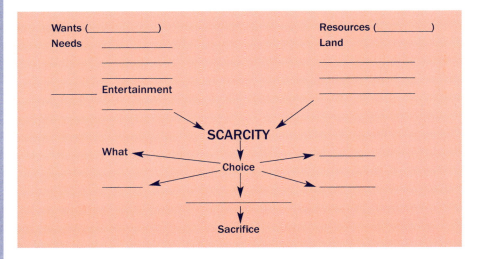

Words to use

Limited, Food, Opportunity, Cost, Where, How, Capital, Shelter, Luxuries, Labour, Who for, Unlimited, TV, Enterprise, Clothing

ACTIVITY TWO

Hurleston Detergents Ltd makes soap and washing powder. It is located in Clevedon. Despite enjoying a 15% market share, the business is no longer profitable and it will be closed down in two months. At present it employs 500 workers. Draw a 'mind map' or 'star diagram' to identify the stakeholders in Hurleston Detergents Ltd and how they will be affected by the closure.

ACTIVITY THREE

Bolton Wanderers Football Club built their stadium, The Reebok, on an area of land, the Red Moss, near the town of Horwich. A shopping centre, the Middlebrook, was developed around the stadium. The Moss was a natural habitat for plant, birds and animals.

Copy and complete the writing frame below to show the likely social benefits and costs of the development. In the lower box, state what other information you would need to decide

Social benefits of The Reebok and Middlebrook	Social costs of The Reebok and Middlebrook

Additional information needed to judge if the development has been good or bad for the local community

ACTIVITIES *cont.*

whether the development of the Reebok and Middlebrook Shopping Centre had been good or bad for the local community.

ACTIVITY FOUR

Copy and complete the table below. Using your knowledge of business objectives (or those given in the Knowledge Hierarchy), state which ones are likely to be appropriate to each organisation.

	Marks and Spencers plc	A new mobile phone provider – in its first year of trading	Bolton Metropolitan Borough Council
Business Objectives			

ACTIVITY FIVE

Using a 'Yellow Pages' or your own knowledge of the area in which you live, write down three examples of businesses in each of the following sectors of the economy: primary, secondary and tertiary.

 QUESTION TYPES TO EXPECT

Questions that ask you to give the meaning and examples of terms such as:

- *Primary, Secondary and Tertiary Sectors*
- *Opportunity Cost*
- *Wants and Resources (Factors of Production)*
- *Consumer and Capital Goods*
- *Stakeholders*
- *Social Costs and Benefits*

More difficult questions that you may be asked:

- *Explain why changes in the employment and output in the primary, secondary and tertiary sectors have occurred.*
- *Analyse employment figures to evaluate the effects on a population of a change in employment in different sectors.*
- *Identify stakeholders in a business and explain how they may be affected by changes in its activity such as its closure or expansion.*
- *Identify the objectives that different types of businesses may have.*
- *Identify the social costs and benefits that may result from some kind of business development such as the development of land for commercial use.*
- *Explain how government and pressure groups may influence the external environment of a business.*

Some examples of these types of questions and student answers are given in the following section. Look carefully at what the question is asking you to do; how the student has answered the question; what the examiner thinks of the answer.

EXTERNAL ENVIRONMENT OF BUSINESS: SPECIMEN QUESTIONS

Question One (Common Question)
The table below shows the changes that have taken place in employment in the three sectors of the economy in the County of Wetland during the period 1960 to 2000.

Year	Primary Sector	Secondary Sector	Tertiary Sector
1960	10,000	120,000	180,000
1980	7000	90,000	230.000
2000	5000	70,000	260,000

a) Describe the main changes that have taken place in employment in each sector of the economy in the period 1960 to 2000. **(6)**

b) Explain why the changes in employment in i) the primary sector and ii) the secondary sector may have occurred during the period 1960 to 2000. **(8)**

c) Explain why the changes in employment in the tertiary sector of the economy of Wetland may have occurred during the period 1960 to 2000. **(6)**

Student Answer

a)   During the period 1960 to 2000 the primary sector has fallen as more machinery is being used. As more machines are used, fewer workers are needed. The secondary sector has also fallen as more people are buying from abroad. This is because it is cheaper, technology is more up-to-date and it is more efficient. The tertiary sector has seen a large increase in the numbers of people employed – in percentage terms the rise is nearly 45%.

b) i)   The primary sector has fallen in employment because more machines and better methods of production are now used – this means that a bigger output of goods can be produced from fewer people. Output per person has also increased because of better techniques of production – for example, genetic engineering has increased the amount that can been grown in one field. No extra workers are needed to make this output.

   ii) The secondary sector has seen a fall in employment also partly because of the use of new technologies such as CAD and CAM. For example, car factories now employ fewer people than they used to because robots do a lot of the work. Also, although the demand for manufactured goods has increased, a lot of these goods are bought from abroad because other countries can produce them more cheaply. For example, a lot of clothing and training shoes are made in the Far East because wages are lower there.

c)   The changes in the tertiary sector are caused by a rise in population, meaning that more teachers and health workers are needed. Also people have more money to spend now because wages have gone up. They can spend this in shops and so more retail workers are needed. People also have more leisure time meaning more leisure parks and centres are being built which requires more workers. Finally, businesses might have placed more importance on customer service as a way of keeping existing customers and gaining new ones. This could lead to a large increase in telephone call centres which themselves need large numbers of workers.

Kirsty

What the Examiner Says

a) Kirsty has misinterpreted the question to an extent. The command word here is 'describe'. Kirsty does describe the changes – at a very basic level for primary and secondary sectors and at a higher level, using percentages, for the tertiary sector. There was no need to 'explain' the changes – this is required in part b) of the question. To gain more marks, Kirsty could have made some comparative comments to the effect that the biggest decline was in the secondary sector and supported the argument with some figures, either for the total changes in employment or (even better) the percentage changes in employment.

Marks awarded – 4 out of 6

b) Kirsty presents a very good answer here. She states reasons why the level of employment in both primary and secondary sectors may have fallen and then illustrates these with clear, appropriate examples.

Marks awarded – 8 out of 8

c) Kirsty discusses a range of possible reasons why there are more jobs in the tertiary sector. She could have made more of some of the points – for example, the increase in incomes along with the increase in leisure time, have resulted in a greater demand for leisure services. It would also have been worth noting that a lot of these services are labour intensive – machinery cannot often be used instead of labour. Still a good answer!

Marks awarded – 6 out of 6

Question Two (Higher Tier)

The table below shows the changes that have taken place in employment in the three sectors of the economy in the County of Wetland during the period 1960 to 2000.

Year	Primary Sector	Secondary Sector	Tertiary Sector
1960	10,000	120,000	180,000
1980	7000	90,000	230,000
2000	5000	70,000	260,000

The External Environment of Business

a) Explain how the importance of the secondary sector in Wetland may have changed in the period 1960 to 2000. **(4)**

b) To what extent are the changes in employment likely to have caused problems for the population of Wetland? Give reasons for your answer. **(8)**

Student Answer

a) Secondary production may be more important because more goods may be being produced in 2000 than in 1960 even though employment has fallen. If output has gone up this will be good for other businesses, both secondary and tertiary, which supply goods and services.

b) The changes in population are likely to cause problems because there will be a lot of people unemployed in the primary and secondary sector. There will also be less money given out in these sectors so the people who work in them will have less money to spend. The changes will also be good because there will be more jobs available in the tertiary sector therefore there will be more money to spend. There will also be more services provided for the people.

Chris

What the Examiner Says

a) The answer here is short – and sweet. Chris has been able to see beyond the fall in employment to suggest that production may not have fallen also. He has also been able to suggest how its production links with the tertiary sector.

Marks awarded – 4 out of 4

b) Chris's approach here is good – he might well have remembered the idea of 'writing frames' because he writes about both problems and advantages and this means that the answer reaches Level 2. The answer is spoilt, though, by a lack of detail and precision and development. For example, from the figures it can be shown that there is more employment in 2000 than in 1980 or in 1960. However, whilst some workers previously employed in the primary and secondary sectors will have been able to find jobs in the expanded tertiary sector, others may not – perhaps because they were too old or incapable of retraining to develop the new skills that they would need. It would also be necessary to know whether their new jobs in the tertiary sector were full or part-time and whether they were lower or higher paid than the jobs they left in the primary and secondary sectors.

This is a level 2 (5–8) – Marks awarded – 5 out of 8

Question Three (a) Common Question b) Higher Tier

Millbank Farm in Wetland produces wheat. Abbey Mills Ltd use wheat to produce flour. Scanlons is a small bakery. Mr Scanlon makes fresh bread daily and sells it to the public in his shop.

a) State which sector of the economy each business is in. **(3)**
b) Explain fully how these businesses are interdependent. **(6)**

Student Answer

a) *Millbank Farm, which produces wheat, is in the primary sector, Abbey Mills is in the secondary sector and Scanlons is in the tertiary sector.*

b) *These businesses are interdependent because Abbey Mills Ltd who are in the secondary sector depend on Millbank Farm who are in the primary sector to produce wheat so that they can produce flour. They need to produce the flour so that Scanlons, which is a small bakery in the tertiary sector, can make the fresh bread every day to sell to the public.*

Danny

What the Examiner Says

a) Danny gets full marks for correctly identifying the sector that each business operates in.

Marks awarded – 3 out of 3

b) The answer tells only half the story! Danny explains how the secondary sector depends on the primary sector and the tertiary sector depends on the secondary. However, the dependency goes both ways. Millbank Farm, as a primary producer, depends on the success of Abbey Mills, the secondary producer, for its market, as Abbey Mills depends on the tertiary producer, Scanlons. To push the line of argument even further, it could be explained that the tertiary sector depends on the primary sector and vice versa

Level One (1–3) – Marks awarded – 3 out of 6

Question Four (Common Question)

State, giving your reasons, **two** objectives that may be suitable for each of the following:

a) Caroline's Cakes   This is a new shop. Caroline wants to set objectives for the first year that she is in business.
b) Wetland County Council.
c) Dearden Pottery Ltd   Dearden Pottery Ltd has been in business for five years. It has established itself in the pottery business in the UK. **(3 × 4 = 12)**

Student Answer

a) *Caroline's shop is so new one of her main objectives for the first year should be survival. Many new businesses fail within just a few months of opening and so surviving the first year would be seen as an achievement. The other important objective would be to make a profit. All businesses need to make a profit in order to be successful, survive and grow. However, Caroline needs to be careful that she does not try to maximise her profits as customers may feel that they are not being treated well and sales could fall.*

b) *Wetland County Council's main objective should be to provide a service because their job is to serve the local community. The only other objective that a council may consider would be to make a profit in order to improve facilities by holding fund raising events.*

c) *Dearden Pottery Ltd has already established itself in the pottery business and has been in business for five years. However they may still see sales growth as an important objective. This does not necessarily mean making more profit, but they could open more shops in different areas, this way the business will grow.*

Kathryn

What the Examiner Says

a) Kathryn correctly identifies the importance of survival for new businesses and provides useful information to emphasise how difficult this is. She also correctly identifies that the business may aim to make a profit and that this would allow further growth in the future. The point about profit maximisation is a good one – though it could have been expressed more clearly. Kathryn could also have developed the point about survival further by, for example, explaining the need to build up regular custom and ensuring that she produces a range of goods that is in demand. However, she did not need to do this – remember, there will usually be several possible answers to get the full marks!

Marks awarded – 4 out of 4

b) Kathryn scores marks for suggesting that the provision of a quality service is an appropriate objective for Wetland County Council and for identifying that it exists to serve the local community. The answer otherwise lacks some clarity. Kathryn needed to explain that as a Council, Wetland does not exist to make a profit. Also, a Council would be unlikely to raise money through fund-raising events – the objective might be to raise revenue in order to finance more or better services. If so, the Council would be likely to raise the money by increasing the Council Tax or seeking grants from central government or, possibly, the European Union.

Marks awarded – 2 out of 4

c) Kathryn makes some relevant points here – the business has become established, it should consider growth. Again, there is some lack of clarity. It is likely that the objective in terms of sales might be expressed in terms of a percentage rate of growth, a target figure in revenue terms or a certain percentage share of the overall market. She might also have explained what she meant by

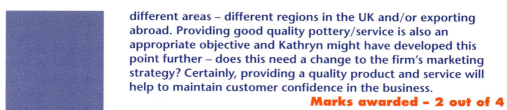

different areas – different regions in the UK and/or exporting abroad. Providing good quality pottery/service is also an appropriate objective and Kathryn might have developed this point further – does this need a change to the firm's marketing strategy? Certainly, providing a quality product and service will help to maintain customer confidence in the business.

Marks awarded – 2 out of 4

Question Five (Higher Tier)

Redborough Council is planning to build a new industrial estate on the edge of the town.

State and explain how stakeholders in the development may be affected if it goes ahead.

(10)

Student Answer

Some stakeholders will be pleased by the development whilst others will not. Those that will be pleased will be:

- *The businesses that will locate on the industrial estate because they will have brand new factories.*
- *Workers who get jobs in the new factories.*
- *Other businesses in the local community will be pleased because they may provide the new businesses with raw materials or with services. For example, a sandwich bar may be able to increase its sales by providing a delivery service to the workers on the new estate. Other local business may also get more sales because the people who work on the new estate may have more income and more money to spend which they spend in local shops and businesses.*
- *The Council, because the businesses will have to pay taxes to the Council.*

The people who will not be pleased will be:

- *The people who live near the new industrial estate – it may be an eyesore, it will mean more traffic in their area of town leading to congestion and noise and air pollution.*
- *Environmental groups may object if the estate is built on agricultural land which makes the area more built up. It is also possible that the land that is built on is the natural habitat for wildlife or for a certain kind of plant.*
- *Some competitors may not be pleased – the new firms may be able to produce at a lower cost because they are in new, modern factories. This may make it difficult for the older firms to compete.*

Ismat

What the Examiner Says

Ismat has produced a very good and very neatly written answer. It identifies both the benefits and the costs of the development – she may have used the writing frame suggested in the Introduction to the book to revise and to plan the work. Not only does she provide a comprehensive list of possible benefits and problems, she develops each point clearly and fully and gives appropriate examples.

Marks awarded – 10 out of 10

Types of Business Organisation

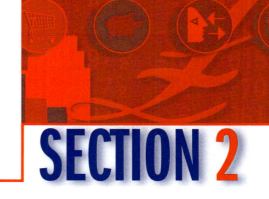

SECTION 2

SOME BASICS

Businesses can be incorporated, as legal bodies such as Private Limited Companies and Public Limited Companies. These types of business are separate from the shareholders who own them. Sole traders and partnerships are unincorporated and are not separate bodies from the people who own them. Unlike these privately funded businesses, organisations in the public sector are funded and owned by the state – local or national government – and are usually service, not profit, motivated.

Revision Material

KNOWLEDGE HIERARCHY: LIST OF THINGS TO KNOW ABOUT TYPES OF BUSINESS ORGANSIATION

This information is intended to provide a quick reminder. Your notes, and the information in the textbook you have used, should provide more detailed information and examples.

Topic	Key Features	Detail	Further Information
Sole Trader e.g. local window cleaner, plumber, etc. • The business is owned by one person • The business may employ one person (the owner) or a number of people	• Unlimited Liability • Unincorporated • Usually small in size • Income Tax paid on profits • Advantages • Disadvantages	• Owner's possessions at risk if declared bankrupt • Owner and business same legal person • Large number of this type of business • Easy to set up • Owner keeps all the profits • Owner makes all the decisions	• Bankrupt = debts greater than assets • Many self-employed people are sole traders • No cost involved

Topic	Key Features	Detail	Further Information
Sole Trader *cont.*		• May not have enough capital for expansion • No continuity if owner dies • May have a skill shortage	• Disadvantages can be overcome by becoming another type of business organisation

Topic	Key Features	Detail	Further Information
Partnership e.g. most doctors, dentists and solicitors • Minimum of 2 and maximum of 20 partners	• Unlimited Liability • Unincorporated • Usually have a Deed of Partnership • Income Tax paid on profits • Advantages • Disadvantages	• Owners' possessions at risk if declared bankrupt • Owners and business same legal person(s) • Legal agreement detailing who is responsible for what • Possibility of Sleeping Partners • Easy to set up • More owners • Profits (and Losses) must be shared • Possibility of disagreements	• Bankrupt = debts greater than assets • Provide capital, not management • Divide management responsibilities • Possibility of more capital available • Deed of Partnership may state how these are to be shared

Topic	Key Feature	Detail	Further Explanation
Private Limited Company (Ltd) e.g. Sainsburys Supermarket Ltd, Derby County Football Club Ltd	• Limited Liability • Incorporated	• Private possessions not at risk in the event of liquidation • Business is separate legal body from shareholders	• Liquidation = paying off debts by selling assets

Topic	Key Feature	Detail	Further Explanation
Private Limited Company (Ltd) *cont.*	• Owned by shareholders	• Board of Directors elected by shareholders • Profit paid to shareholders as dividend	• Election takes place at AGM • Some profit may be retained
	• Corporation Tax paid on profits		
	• Advantage	• Can raise capital through sales of shares	
	• Disadvantages	• Limited finance available through share sale • Some financial information has to be made public	• Cannot sell shares to raise finance via the Stock Market

Topic	Key Feature	Detail	Further Explanation
Public Limited Company (plc) e.g. Marks and Spencer plc, Tesco plc	• Limited Liability	• Private possessions not at risk in the event of liquidation	• Liquidation = paying off debts by selling assets
	• Incorporated	• Business is separate legal body from shareholders	
	• Usually a very large company		
	• Corporation Tax paid on profits		
	• Must have issued share capital in excess of £50 000		
	• Advantage	• Can raise large amounts of finance	• Share can be offered for sale to the general public as a means of raising finance
	• Disadvantages	• Business can be taken over if sufficient shares are obtained • No privacy	• Financial information has to be available for public inspection

Topic	Key Feature	Detail	Further Explanation
Other Types of Business Organisation	• **Franchise** e.g. Benetton, McDonalds, Body Shop	• Can trade as any of the four types of business organisation • Franchises are a type of marketing arrangement	• Franchisee provides advertising, advice, a tried and tested product • Franchise is often a well-known name • Franchisee pays a Royalty in return and can be expensive to set up
	• **Multinational** e.g. Ford Motor Company, Unilever, Nokia	• Usually very large businesses	• Multinational companies located in more than one country • Located near to market • Often lower manufacturing costs in other countries • Save on high transport costs to distant markets • Economies of large scale production may be lost by having several manufacturing facilities
	• **Holding Company** e.g. Dixons Group plc, Centrica plc	• Own other businesses • Usually large	• May gain economies of scale • May trade under different names or brand names • Larger market can be targeted • Easier to establish new businesses as markets change
	• **Co-operative** Producer/ Manufacturer	• Co-operatives popular for agricultural businesses where machinery can be shared	• Costs can be shared

Topic	Key Feature	Detail	Further Explanation
Other Types of Business Organisation *cont*	• **Co-operative** *cont*	• Some manufacturing businesses operate as worker co-operatives • Workers are also the owners of the business • Often set up by workers to protect jobs when a business is faced with closure	• Workers make the decisions

PUTTING IT IN CONTEXT

Sole trader businesses are suitable for small-scale operations where the capital needed can be provided out of the owner's (and probably his or her family's) savings, supplemented perhaps by a loan from a bank. Graham Thompson started a plumbing business as a sole trader. After four successful years, during which he developed a reputation locally for providing a high quality service, Graham wanted to expand the business so that it provided a wider range of services for business and domestic customers.

Graham needed to move to larger premises, to employ electricians and decorators and provide additional vehicles for these workers to use.

Graham took on a *partner*, partly to provide some of the additional capital needed but also to give him help in managing the business. The new partner, Ashley Hanson, had been an office manager. Ashley now ran the administration side of the business. When the partnership was formed, Graham drew up a *Deed of Partnership* clarifying how much capital each partner had provided and how any profit would be distributed, as well as stating the responsibilities of each partner. He knew it would help prevent possible conflict in the future.

Graham's sister, Maria, had also gone into business. With her husband, she had applied to run a Body Shop *franchise*. They decided that, in the light of their limited business experience,

41

the advice they would receive, the marketing expertise and the tried and tested product range the franchiser would provide, it would be worth the loss of control and the expensive royalty charge they would have to pay. Maria and her husband had also decided that, with set-up costs of £350,000 financed by their own savings, a mortgage, bank loan and generous trade credit terms from the franchiser to purchase stock, they needed *limited liability* status. They decided that trading as a *private limited company* was the only alternative as the business was not large enough to make it worthwhile becoming a *public limited company*. Their business would not need the large injection of funds that public limited companies are able to obtain by selling to large numbers of shareholders. Being a private limited company meant that they did not need to make shares available through the Stock Exchange and so, as the two main shareholders, Maria and her husband would be able to maintain control. They knew that people would have access to their accounts if they wanted it.

One of the first things that Maria did when setting up the business was to draw up an *organisation chart* showing who is responsible for what. Whilst the business did not employ many workers, it allowed Maria to double check that she had people in place to do all the different jobs that were necessary. She also knew that the managers would be clear about for whom they were responsible and the workers clear about to whom they were responsible. Although the business was organised as a hierarchy, with her as the Managing Director, it was not a very tall organisation and this meant that communication between people in the different layers was not too complicated.

 # ACTIVITIES

ACTIVITY ONE
Devise a *mind map* showing the advantages and disadvantages of operating a business as a Sole Trader.

ACTIVITY TWO
a) Draw an organisation chart for any one of the following: your School; a business you have studied; a business for which you have worked. The starting point may be the person in charge or the owner of the business.
- How many different departments or sections does your organisation have?
- What are the names of the staff?
- Do you know their job titles?
- Who are their line managers?
- What type of business organisation is it?

b) How and why might the organisation chart need to change as the business changes?

ACTIVITY THREE
List some possible reasons for and against a business considering changing from a:

- Sole Trader to a Partnership
- Partnership to a Private Limited Company
- Private Limited Company to a Public Limited Company

ACTIVITY FOUR
The table below gives clues to some of the terms used when considering the key features of different types of business organisation. See if you can work out the answer to each clue.

ACTIVITIES *cont.*

Clue	Term
Helps protect your personal possessions if your business becomes insolvent.	
Usually paid to Shareholders twice a year – if you are lucky!	
Type of business where the owner keeps all the profits.	
There can be a maximum of 20 of these.	
This type of business is usually found in several countries.	
Usually elected by Shareholders at the Annual General Meeting	
If over £50,000 of shares have been issued, the business is probably one of these.	
This type of business can't sell them to the General Public in order to raise finance.	
The name of the payment made to the franchiser for the right to use a business name.	
A part owner of a business who invests money in it but takes no part in its day-to-day running.	
This type of business allows other businesses it owns to operate under different names.	
Two forms of business have to make these available for public inspection.	

 QUESTION TYPES TO EXPECT

Questions that ask you to give the meaning and examples of terms such as:

- *Limited and Unlimited Liability*
- *Insolvency and Bankruptcy*
- *Ltd and PLC*
- *Incorporated and Unincorporated*
- *Board of Directors*
- *Shareholders*
- *Franchise, Franchisee, Franchiser, Royalty*
- *Multinational or Holding Company*

and many other business terms, are frequently asked by examiners.

Other questions may ask you to:

- *give or explain a certain number of advantages or disadvantages of one or two of the different types of business organisation.*
- *give or explain a number of key features about a particular form of business organisation.*
- *select, from a list, features which are appropriate to a particular form of business organisation.*

More difficult questions, which are likely to require a detailed response, may ask you to:

- advise or evaluate the appropriateness of a particular form of business organisation, based on some information which has been provided.
- recommend, giving reasons, appropriate ways for a given type of business to obtain additional finance.
- consider whether it would be better to operate as a franchise or as an independent business.

Some examples of these types of questions and student answers are given in the following section. Look carefully at what the question is asking you to do; how the student has answered the question; what the examiner thinks of the answer.

TYPES OF BUSINESS ORGANISATION: SPECIMEN QUESTIONS

Question One (Higher Tier)

James Brown has recently inherited some money which he wants to invest by setting up his own business. He has decided that a vacant shop unit near to where he lives would be ideal for a fast food restaurant and, given that he has worked for Pizza Supreme for four years as a restaurant manager, he will start a take-away pizza business. However, he cannot decide whether to set up as an independent business or become part of a well-known pizza franchise.

Discuss the advantages and disadvantages of each option. Giving reasons, say which one you would recommend James to do. **(12)**

Student Answer

If James were to set up as an independent business, money would need to be spent on employing staff, promoting the business, as well as purchasing a shop unit. This means a considerable amount of initial outlay would be needed and also a considerable amount of risk would be involved.

If James were to buy a well-known pizza franchise, the initial outlay on a unit for the shop equipment would not be needed. The company would already be established and therefore there would be no need for promotion. The main problem with a franchise is that there would be less flexibility.

If, for example, a franchise of Domino Pizza is purchased, the same standards are usually required. This means product ranges must be the same and if demand for a certain product is higher then promotions must be franchise-wide.

If James purchased a shop unit and set up as a sole trader he has far fewer limitations to his business operation. After he established himself with a name and certain style of pizza he would be able to be far more profitable.

Matthew

What the Examiner Says

Matthew has correctly identified the high initial cost of starting a business from scratch and the risky nature of such a venture.

Unfortunately, Matthew does not fully understand how a franchise operates and has made no mention of the fact that an initial payment to the franchiser would be required and an on-going royalty payment probably based on the profitability of the business. Start-up capital would also still be required to buy equipment and obtain suitable premises.

No mention has been made of the advantages of trading under a well-known brand name other than to recognise that all franchises present a common format and service standard to the consumer.

A consideration of the extent of competition which a new business might face and how it could establish itself in the market would have helped the quality of Matthew's answer. Matthew might also have made use of the information provided about the experience of James as a manager of a Pizza Supreme shop.

The question has not been fully answered as Matthew has failed to do what the question asks – **make a recommendation**. A series of facts has been provided for the reader to make up their own mind.

Matthew might have achieved a Level 2 (5–8 marks) answer worth 7 of the 12 marks available. A recommendation, with reasons, would have been necessary to achieve a Level 3 (9–12 marks) answer.

Question Two (Common Question)

Large companies can sometimes experience problems which are not a problem to smaller companies. Shown below are two possible problems:

- communication difficulties
- increased costs of production

Explain, giving examples, how these problems may affect a company. Give reasons for your answers.
(12)

Student Answer

Large companies experience problems which are not a problem to smaller companies because of their different hierarchical structures. The different types of hierarchy can cause communication problems. Smaller companies tend not to have communication problems because there are fewer people working there. Also with larger companies, there are different departments such as marketing, human resources, finance, etc. These departments may not communicate which may cause problems overall. However, through simple communication such as meetings and email these problems may be overcome.

For a large company to have increased costs of production it would mean increased costs for the customer. Customers may then start shopping at smaller companies where it is likely that they may then start to expand. By expanding they are creating more competition for the larger companies which will want to keep their share of the market. Also this may stop the company from achieving economies of scale. This may not allow the business to expand. Increased costs of production can also lead to a loss of jobs. This may cause the company to downsize.

Charlotte

What the Examiner Says

Charlotte has, quite correctly, attempted to organise the answer into two separate parts, making it easier for the examiner to mark. This is important, as a clearly set out answer is an important requirement for the exam.

Unfortunately, both parts of the answer are very confused and fall well short of actually answering the question which has been set. In the first part, there is clearly some understanding that larger organisations will have more of a hierarchical structure but there is no mention of the length of the Chain of Command or the width of the Span of Control. Both of these can contribute to communication problems in terms of the time it may take for information to be passed on or the clarity of the information received by the end user. There is though, recognition that smaller businesses with fewer employees usually have fewer communication problems because of the relative ease with which information can be passed on. Charlotte could have mentioned more than just email and meetings as methods which might go some way to improving communication. Examples of why and how these methods might help could have been given.

In the second part of the answer there is a great deal of confusion. Terms such as economies of scale are used but without showing any real understanding of what the term means and how this type of information could have been used to answer the question. Charlotte has correctly identified that increased costs do affect the selling price of a product or service which has to be paid by the consumer. As a result of this, consumers may choose to go elsewhere. There is no mention of the way in which businesses attempt to control costs nor is there any mention of the different types of costs involved.

This candidate has probably done sufficient to earn a Level 2 (5–8 marks) mark – but only just. There is some understanding but there are too many inaccurate and poorly explained points. A mark of only 5 out of 12 is likely to have been awarded.

Question Three (Common Question)

Speedy Block, a partnership specialising in block paving for patios and drives, has been in business for just over two years. It has been trading very successfully and the two brothers who run the business are considering converting the company to a private limited company.

a) Explain, giving reasons, which type of business organisation you would
recommend for Speedy Block. **(8)**

b) Speedy Block has become a successful business in a short time. Not all new
businesses are successful. Discuss the factors which might cause a new business
to fail. **(8)**

Student Answer

*a)   There are pros and cons of becoming an incorporated business. If the
business remains a partnership, it will face unlimited liability. This is a
considerable risk despite the recent success of the business. Being
unincorporated also means having to make all decisions facing the business. Security,
then, is the principle reason for becoming incorporated. Such a move would enable the
business to have limited liability. Conversely, it is not possible to use shares as a means of
raising funds; private limited company shares may not be advertised for sale outside the
business if the business were to decide on this form of organisation. I would not
recommend the business attempt conversion to a public limited company as the business
would have to sell over £50,000 worth of shares before it could start trading.*

*b)   Not all businesses are successful. There are many factors which can affect the success of
a business, particularly a new one. Such things as the degree of competition in the
market in which the business is trading; the amount of work or orders it receives; the
way in which the business controls its costs; the price it charges in relation to the costs of
doing something will all have an effect on the success of the business. New businesses
have particular problems. One of the most significant will be establishing itself in the
market place and getting its name known. Without this it is unlikely to get sufficient
work. Many new businesses are also set up through loans. These debts have to be repaid
with interest and these businesses have to be particularly hard working and profitable if
they are to generate sufficient finance to meet the repayments. Establishing a reputation
will also be important for a new business and this can be difficult to do until work has
been completed for customers.*

Louise

What the Examiner Says

a) **Louise has correctly identified one of the key problems facing
businesses when deciding on the type of business organisation –
limited or unlimited liability. However, no detail has been given as
to the advantages and disadvantages of this key feature other
than to make some reference to security. This particular point
should have been developed and explained fully in terms of the
effects on the personal possessions of the owner(s) of a business
in the event of bankruptcy/liquidation.**

**There are, of course, other issues relating to the type of business
organisation to choose and these should have been discussed
more fully. However, Louise does have some understanding of the
types of business organisation available but should have given
the advantages and disadvantages of each type of business
organisation referred to in the question. This would have helped**

when making a recommendation – as required by the question. The question did not require any reference to be made to Public Limited Companies but it did require some consideration of the relevance of remaining in business as a Partnership.

Marks awarded – 4 out of 8

b) This is a good, detailed answer, which considers a large number of factors which are likely to have an effect on the success of a business. The candidate has also attempted to relate these factors to the problems which new businesses, in particular, are likely to face.

Marks awarded – 7 out of 8

Question Four (Higher Tier)

Shown below is some information for HOP IT plc, an extremely successful low cost airline. Using this information, and any other you have available, answer the questions which follow.

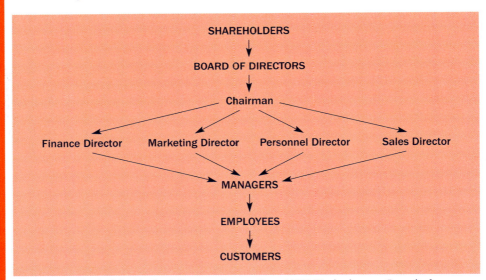

a) Explain why Public Limited Companies, such as HOP IT plc, have a Board of Directors. **(6)**

b) Suggest and explain ONE problem to HOP IT plc of trading as a Public Limited Company. **(4)**

c) Explain why shareholders might have invested money into a company such as HOP IT plc. **(4)**

d) Name TWO groups of Stakeholders in HOP IT plc and suggest why they have an interest in the company. **(8)**

Student Answer

a) *Because a Public Limited company has limited liability and so if the business gets into financial difficulties, it would be the Board of Directors that would lose their house, etc. to pay off the debts. This is instead of the chairman or shareholders.*

b) *Public Limited Companies can't advertise their shares on the stock market. This reduces the number of possible investors for the company and makes it difficult for them to generate money.*

c) *They are a low cost airline so customers will like using them to travel. Therefore, income will increase and the higher the income and lower the output, the greater the profit. Dividends may therefore increase.*

d) *Passengers – they want a quick comfortable journey for a low price and a low risk factor.*

Staff – they are looking to give passengers a good service so their chances of promotion are increased. They want loyal customers so sales revenue and net profit will increase. Therefore chance of pay rises are greater.

Nisha

What the Examiner Says

a) Nisha has not answered the question and clearly does not have any understanding of limited liability. Limited Liability is irrelevant in terms of answering the question. No mention has been made about how the Board of Directors is elected by shareholders to make important decisions about the direction that the business will take and to oversee, on behalf of shareholders, the operation of the business.

Marks awarded – 0 out of 6

b) Whilst Nisha correctly identifies that shares are sold as a means of raising finance she has incorrectly stated that **Public** Limited Companies are unable to do this. Perhaps a more appropriate answer might have been to identify the problems regarding the possibility of a take-over if one person or organisation obtains a large number of shares. Secondly, she could have mentioned the fact that a plc needs to make financial information available to the general public which may be of advantage to competitors.

Marks awarded – 2 out of 4

c) Nisha has correctly identified that the demand for low cost air travel is increasing leading to an increase in income for the business. Nisha has also correctly identified that this may lead to an increase in profits leading to larger dividends for shareholders. However, there is some confusion with regard to output and costs.

Marks awarded – 3 out of 4

Question Five (Common Question)

Shown below is the Organisation Chart for Highfield Holding plc. Use the information in the chart, and any other information, to answer the questions which follow.

a) Explain the difference between a Holding Company and a Subsidiary Company. **(5)**

b) Recommend to Highfield Holdings plc whether or not it is a good idea to let its businesses trade under their own names. **(9)**

Student Answer

a) If the subsidiary company were trading under the more well-known name of Highfield Holdings they will gain a greater share of the market at a quicker rate. Clearly, the businesses will benefit from trading as Highfield Holdings – using their reputation to gain a competitive advantage.

b) There are obviously a number of advantages and disadvantages for Highfield Holdings in allowing its subsidiary companies to trade under their own names. It would be advantageous for Highfield Holdings as it would allow specific businesses to gain a reputable trading name in their particular markets. For example, Price Right Ltd, is a fashion retailer and it may be argued that Highfield Holdings would not have the same 'fashionable' appeal to consumers. Highfield Holdings must ensure that they choose the appropriate trading name in order to gain a competitive advantage over competitors.

Highfield Holdings will benefit from allowing the individual companies to trade under their own names as this will allow each individual business to target different market segments. In addition, it can be argued that allowing each business to trade under their own name will reduce risk. For example, if one subsidiary company were to fail or make a considerable loss, then the reputation of Highfield Holdings would be less affected than if it were to trade under its own name. The reduction of risk of this type may be useful in a volatile market such as fashion.

However, Highfield Holdings must also consider the drawbacks of allowing its subsidiary companies to trade under their own names. For example, Trendy Fashions may be struggling to gain a hold in the market. It may be argued that a well-known name with a reputation for quality may stand a better chance of establishing itself in the market.

Ben

What the Examiner Says

a) Ben has not answered the question. There is no mention of the fact that a Holding Company owns a Subsidiary company but allows it to trade under its **own** name. A more detailed response might have referred to the fact that an investor wishing to buy shares in, for example Trendy Fashions Ltd, would have to buy shares in Highfield Holdings as it is this business which probably owns most, if not all the shares, in Trendy Fashions Ltd.

Marks awarded – 0 out of 5

b) This is a detailed answer with many relevant points which go a long way to answering the question. However, Ben has not actually made a **firm** recommendation as required by the question.

Whilst this may be a Level 3 (7–9 marks) answer, Ben has only just provided sufficient information for the award of Level 3.

Marks awarded – 7 out of 9

Question Six (Common Question)

Bill Jones, a Sole Trader, has been running a small but successful electronic circuit board manufacturing business for several years. At the moment he has five employees.

His accountant has advised him to consider converting to a Limited Liability form of business organisation. He does not know what to do and has asked for your help.

Advise Bill of the advantages and disadvantages of staying as a Sole Trader or converting to a Limited Liability business. **(12)**

Student Answer

As a Sole Trader and owner of a small business there are a number of advantages. He has sole ownership of the business and therefore full control of the way in which it is run. He can decide the hours of work, shift patterns and wage rates for workers, etc. If he converted to a limited company, unless he kept all the shares in the business, he may lose control to other shareholders.

There are a number of drawbacks to operating as a Sole Trader. There may be no one to cover his position should he fall ill. He holds full responsibility for the running of the business and should it get into trouble financially any debts may have to be paid by Bill even if this means having to sell his personal possessions. With limited liability, this element of risk is removed and he would only stand to lose his initial investment if the business were to get into financial trouble.

Although there is more risk running as a Sole Trader, it would be better for this small business to stay unchanged. The business is successful and in the technology market, which has a high level of investment and is continuously expanding, the risk of running into trouble is minimal. Currently it might be better for Mr Jones to stay in full control and he should only consider converting to limited liability if the business expands significantly and/or takes on more risk.

Katie

What the Examiner Says

Katie has offered a lot of sound advise, as required by the question. A recommendation, backed up by reasons, has also been made. The answer, perhaps, dwells a little too much on the aspect of limited versus unlimited liability. Some consideration might have been given to the problems which many small businesses face when seeking to raise additional finance. However, Katie has recognised the key advantages/disadvantages of the Sole Trader form of business organisation. Some mention should also have been made about some of the problems that exist in becoming a Limited Company. For instance, the need to make some financial information available to the public which may be of use to competitors.

This is a good answer and is clearly worth Level 3 (9–12 marks)

Marks awarded – 10 out of 12

Accounting and Finance

SECTION 3

SOME BASICS

Money is the lifeblood of a business. Too little, and the business is in danger of stopping. Too much, and the business may not use it as effectively as it should. As a result, most businesses spend a lot of time managing money, making sure that there is enough of it at the right time. Much of this work is done by accountants who prepare detailed financial statements which help the managers of the business to make decisions.

Whilst not all businesses need be profit-making, most of them are. Knowing whether the business is operating at a profit or a loss is very important. However, some businesses fail, not because they are unprofitable, but because they simply run out of money. Customers may not have paid for their goods; too much money may be tied up in stock; bills are more than anticipated or not enough has been sold. On the other hand, a business will fail if it cannot sell its products or services at a profit.

Revision Material

KNOWLEDGE HIERARCHY: LIST OF THINGS TO KNOW ABOUT TYPES OF BUSINESS ORGANSIATION

This information is intended to provide a quick reminder. Your notes, and the information in the textbook you have used, should provide more detailed information and examples.

Topic	Key Features	Detail	Further Information
Sources of finance e.g. Share Issue; Hire Purchase; Debenture	• Large number of different sources	• Type of finance used depends on a range of factors • The amount required, the length of time and the cost are all important considerations	• Factors include the type of business wishing to use the finance; the use to which the finance will be put

Topic	Key Features	Detail	Further Information
Sources of finance *cont.*	• Two basic types of finance – Internal and External	• Internal finance comes from within the business	• Several different types, e.g. Retained Profit; selling assets for cash
		• Advantages	• Money does not have to be paid back • No interest to be paid
		• Disadvantage	• Opportunity cost involved
		• External finance is provided from outside the business	• Many different types, e.g. loan; mortgage
		• Advantage	• Successful businesses find it easier to obtain this type of finance
		• Disadvantages	• Usually a cost involved • A form of security often needed
	• Combination of different sources of finance often used	• Helps overcome or reduce some of the disadvantages	

Topic	Key Features	Detail	Further Information
Profit Money left over from Sales Revenue once all costs have been paid for	• Key objective of most businesses • Not all businesses are profit-making	• Examples of non-profit making businesses are charities	
	• Several different types of profit	• Gross Profit, Net Profit, Operating Profit are all calculated by business	
	• Size of the profit made can be used to judge success	• Profit comparisons can be made with previous years • Profit performance can be compared to other (similar) businesses	• Ratio analysis used to compare performance • Gross Profit to Sales and Net Profit to Sales ratios used to compare performance

Topic	Key Features	Detail	Further Information
Profit *cont.*			• Profit Margin or Mark-up are also used by businesses
	• Large number of factors which can influence the size of the profit made	• Fierce competition may reduce sales, prices and therefore profit • Poor cost control may reduce profit	
	• Profit is often re-invested in the business	• Retained profit is used to help fund the activities of the business • Some profit paid to shareholders	• Dividends are a payment made to shareholders from profits not retained by the business
	• Loss-making businesses rarely survive for long		
	• New businesses often find it hard to make a profit in the first few years of trading	• New businesses have high start-up costs	• New businesses usually need to buy a lot of equipment

Topic	Key Features	Detail	Further Information
Cash Flow Needs to be managed to ensure the business does not run out of cash	• The flow of money in and out of a business	• Businesses attempt to forecast the flow of money in and out of the business	• A forecast covers a particular time period – usually a month • Forecasted income minus forecasted expenditure shows how much money the business might have available
		• Some businesses with seasonal activities may have a difficult cash flow to manage	• Ice cream sellers and fireworks manufacturers have sales which fall at particular times • Supermarkets tend to have a fairly even flow of cash as people need food all the year round

Topic	Key Features	Detail	Further Information
Cash Flow *cont*	• Cash Flow is not a profit calculation	• Surplus cash represents a positive cash balance • A negative cash balance may mean the business has to take action	• A business needs to use its cash surplus effectively • Delaying payment, selling more or chasing up debts may help the cash position • Borrowing; cutting costs; selling more goods may help the business overcome a temporary negative cash balance

Topic	Key Features	Detail	Further Information
The final Accounts of a Business Two main documents – the Trading, Profit and Loss Account; The Balance Sheet. Documents are completed quarterly, half-yearly or yearly	• Trading Profit and Loss Account used to calculate profit or loss • Balance Sheet states what the business owns and owes • Accounting information details exactly what has happened to the business over a period of time	• Accounts are read by a large number of interested stakeholders • Assets of a business must always equal the Liabilities • Information in the documents can be used to compare performance by using Ratio analysis • Recognising the trend over time is important • Comparisons can be made with other businesses • Each Ratio has an 'ideal' answer	• Trading Profit and Loss Account shows the different types of profit and what has happened to it • Balance Sheet lists all the Assets and Liabilities of the business • Balance Sheet also shows where the business has got its money from and how it has been used • Assets and Liabilities are listed according to liquidity • Current Ratio ideal answer is around 2 • Acid Test ideal answer is between 0.8 and 1

Topic	Key Features	Detail	Further Information
The final Accounts of a Business *cont*	• Ratios used to compare if the business is getting better or worse over time	• Results either side of the ideal answer indicate that the business is not managing its resources effectively	• Both ratios measure the liquidity of the business
		• Working Capital is another test of how much money the business has available for its day-to-day needs	• A negative Working Capital figure indicates that the business is in danger of running out of cash for day-to-day activities
		• Return on Capital Employed (ROCE) is yet another financial measure	• ROCE compares the relationship between the profit made and the amount of money (capital) needed to generate it

PUTTING IT IN CONTEXT

Sam Brown's garden services business – Garden Designs Ltd – is a real success story. Sam started the business as a sole trader just over five years ago. It had very little equipment and only enough work to employ Sam. It is now a very successful and profitable private limited company employing four full-time and several part-time workers. One of the best decisions she made when she started the business was to take her friend's advise to use the services of an accountant. The accountant would be able to prepare her financial statements and offer business advice.

As the business grew in size and needed more equipment, Sam's accountant was able to provide information about different *sources of finance* which might be available to help purchase the new equipment. Sam had not realised that only certain sources of finance were available to different types of business, nor had she realised the *costs* and *drawbacks* involved.

When she first started out in business, Sam had not realised how important it was for her to manage her *cash flow*. Some jobs, which she was given, needed large quantities of materials which had to be bought before starting. If the customer was a little slow in paying for the work Sam sometimes found that she was in danger of running out of money even though she knew that the prices she was charging more than covered the cost of the materials and her time. Sam quickly learned that getting *trade credit* from her suppliers, therefore delaying payment for goods, and making sure that customers paid promptly, helped to make sure that the business did not have cash-flow problems.

One of the most important jobs which Sam's accountant did for her business was to prepare her *final accounts*. Sam's *Trading*, *Profit and Loss Account* showed her exactly how much business she had done during the year and how much *profit* had been made. She could see clearly the *Sales Revenue* the business had earned and the *costs* involved in running the business. Her accountant explained, using a technique called *Ratio Analysis*, how to compare the information from one year with previous years so that Sam could see how much progress the businesses was making. Sam's *Balance Sheet* showed her *how much the business was worth* and *how much money was owed* by it. The Balance Sheet showed the value of all the *assets* and liabilities which the business had. Again, by comparing the information contained in the Balance Sheet with that from previous years it was possible to measure how financially secure her business was.

Sam now really understood why it was so important to pay such close attention to the finances of her business and what good advice her friend had given her.

ACTIVITIES

ACTIVITY ONE

The table below shows the main ratios used to compare financial performance. Complete the table by writing in the formula for each ratio and explain what the ratio tells you about the financial circumstances of the business.

Ratio	Formula	The purpose for which the ratio is used
Gross Profit to Sales		
Net Profit to Sales		
Acid Test		
Current Ratio		
Working Capital		
Return on Capital Employed (ROCE)		

ACTIVITIES *cont.*

ACTIVITY TWO

Work out the answers to the following questions which are based on the contents of a Trading Profit and Loss Account:

a) What does Sales Revenue minus Cost of Sales equal?
b) What is the amount of stock which a business has at the beginning of a trading period known as?
c) What is this amount of stock (referred to in Question b) known as at the end of the previous trading period?
d) What is subtracted from Gross Profit to calculate Net Profit?
e) What is the name given to the payment made from profits to the owners of a Limited Company?
f) What is money kept by the business, to pay for new equipment, known as?
g) All businesses have to pay tax on the profits which they make. What is the name given to the tax paid on profits by:
  i) Sole Traders and Partnerships?
  ii) Limited Companies?
h) Why might the Sales Revenue of a business change from one year to another?
i) Prepare a *Mind Map* showing the uses to which a Trading Profit and Loss Account is put by most businesses.

ACTIVITY THREE

Complete the following Balance Sheet by replacing **XXXXX** with the correct words or figures.

Balance Sheet for Garden Design Ltd as at 31 March 2003

	£	£	£
XXXXX Assets			
Plant and Equipment		25 000	
Vehicles		30 000	55 000
XXXXX Assets			
Stock	5 000		
Debtors	20 000		
Bank	15 000	40 000	
Current XXXXX			
Overdraft	3 000		
Trade Creditors	15 000	XXXXX	
Net XXXXX Capital			XXXXX
NET XXXXX EMPLOYED			<u>XXXXX</u>
Shareholders Funds			
Ordinary Shares		30 000	
Reserves and XXXXX Profit		45 000	XXXXX
Long Term Liabilities			
Bank Loan		2 000	2 000
XXXXX EMPLOYED			<u>77 000</u>

ACTIVITIES *cont.*

ACTIVITY FOUR

Using a grid outline similar to the one below:

a) List all the different sources of finance which you can think of.
b) Place a ✓ in the columns to the right of the source of finance to indicate whether that source is likely to be used by a particular type of business.
c) In the last column, suggest a use to which this source of finance may be put.

An example has been done for you.

Source of Finance	Sole Trader	Partnership	Private Limited Company	Public Limited Company	Example(s) of use of Finance
Sale of shares to the general public				✓	Capital is needed to finance an expansion programme or the purchase of another business

ACTIVITY FIVE

Make a copy of the following Cash Flow Outline.

	January £	February £	March £	April £	May £	June £
Opening Balance b/f						
INCOME:						
TOTAL INCOME						

ACTIVITIES *cont.*

	January £	February £	March £	April £	May £	June £
EXPENDITURE:						
TOTAL EXPENDITURE						
Closing Balance c/f						

a) Use the following information to draw up a Cash Flow Forecast for Garden Designs Ltd. The business starts off the time period with a balance of £1000. It expects sales in January to be £6000, rising by £2000 each month until April when sales peak and remain constant for the rest of the time period.

   Expenditure is much more variable. Wages are expected to be constant for the first three months at £5000 and then increase to £6000 followed by two months at £7000. Insurance of £3000 is due in February and Accountancy Fees of £1000 are paid in April. Fuel costs are £100 per month except for May and June when the fuel bill is expected to double. Material costs are low in January at £1000 rising to £2000 in February. The monthly materials bill for the rest of the time period is expected to be £3000.

b) Explain possible reasons for the expected Cash Flow deficit in the early part of the year. Explain why the business may not be too concerned about the forecast deficit.

c) Explain why the business expects to have so much cash available at the end of the time period and why this may be important for this type of business.

d) Explain how businesses forecast their expected income and expenditure.

e) Complete an *Image Chain* detailing the sequence of events for the preparation and use of a Cash Flow Forecast such as the one you have just completed in a) above.

 QUESTION TYPES TO EXPECT

Questions that ask you to give the meaning and examples of terms such as:

- *Fixed and Current Assets*
- *Current and Long Term Liabilities*
- *Gross, Net and Retained Profit*
- *Sales Revenue*

- *Cash Flow*
- *Internal and External Finance*
- *Different Sources of Finance*
- *Opportunity Cost*
- *Shareholders Funds and Dividends*

and many other business terms, are frequently asked by the examiners.

Using numerical data is an essential part of understanding accounting and finance. You should therefore expect to find a reasonable number of questions containing a numerical content. They are designed to test your ability to use, apply and evaluate numerical and financial data.

Numerical and financial data may be presented in a variety of ways. Pie charts, bar graphs, tables and financial documents are just some of the ways. Expect to find these ways in an examination question paper.

Examples of how numerical skills may be tested include:

- *calculating how much Sales Revenue, Profit, Expenditure or some other figure has changed from one year to another either as a simple figure, or as a percentage change.*
- *estimating how much additional finance the business may require to complete a project is another possibility.*
- *working out some of the missing figures from a Cash Flow Forecast; Trading, Profit and Loss Account; Balance Sheet.*
- *using Ratio Analysis to analyse the financial information of a business.*

Other questions, which may require detailed answers, might ask you to pass comment or provide some form of advice to the business. For instance:

- *Using the information available advise the business how it may overcome a particular problem.*
- *Evaluate the appropriateness of a particular course of action based on the information available.*
- *Recommend, giving reasons, alternative ways of financing the business.*

Some examples of these types of questions and student answers are given in the following section. Look carefully at what the question is asking you to do; how the student has answered the question; what the examiner thinks of the answer.

ACCOUNTING AND FINANCE: SPECIMEN QUESTIONS

Question One (Higher Tier)
The following table contains a summary of the information contained in the accounts of Bowton Engineering plc for the years ending 2001 and 2002. Read the information carefully and use it to help answer the questions which follow.

	2001	2002
Sales Revenue	£400m	£500m
Gross Profit	£80m	£120m
Net Profit	£20m	£25m
Dividend per Share	10p	11p

a) Discuss the factors which may have caused an increase in the Sales Revenue between 2001 and 2002. **(6)**

b) Comment on the performance of the business in 2002 compared to 2001. **(8)**

Student Answer

a)   An increase in sales revenue could be due to an increase in sales or a fall in costs which could be the result of economies of scale such as bulk buying. Or, an increase in selling price and a constant, or slight drop in sales, would result in an increased sales revenue.

b) Overall business performance in 2002 was much improved on that of 2001. As sales revenue has increased by £100m from £400m to £500m which led to an increased gross profit of £120m rather than £80m in 2001. This increased gross profit therefore led to an increase in the net profit by £5m from £20m to £25m which led to a higher dividend payment of 11p rather than 10p per share which had been paid previously. Therefore, Bowton Engineering had a much better year in 2002 than in 2001 which could have been due to many factors, e.g. an increase in sales; fall in production costs; increased selling price or an increased efficiency level.

Paul

What the Examiner Says

a) **Whilst this may appear a brief answer, Paul has made a good attempt at answering the question. The reference to a fall in costs is irrelevant as costs would have no impact on the sales revenue earned by a business. Paul has recognised that even a slight drop in the number of items sold, with an increased selling price, could probably lead to an increase in the sales revenue. Making reference to elasticity could have extended this part of the answer. Some mention could have been made about the effect of competition on sales or the popularity of the product(s) being sold.**

This is a Level 2 answer (4–6 marks)
Marks awarded – 4 out of 6

b) **Paul's analysis of the financial information effectively restates the information in the table in text form. Some suggestions have been made to explain the differences in the figures between 2001 and 2002. What Paul has failed to do is to recognise that a ratio analysis comparison needs to be made between Gross Profit and Sales (24% compared to 20%) and Net Profit and Sales (5% compared with 5%) so that a more accurate comparison can be made between performances in 2002 compared with 2001. Had this been done, the conclusions drawn by Paul might have been different.**

Other percentage comparisons could also have been made by calculating the percentage increase in Sales Revenue (25%) and comparing this with the percentage increase in both Gross Profit

(50%) and Net Profit (25%). Had this been done, comment could have been made on the increase in sales resulting in different percentage increases in the two measures of profit. Some form of explanation should have been offered as to why this was the case. For instance, costs of running the business have risen at the same rate as sales but costs of buying goods for re-sale have fallen, possibly because of economies of scale.

This is a Level 1 answer (1–3 marks)
Marks awarded – 3 out of 8

Question Two (Common Question)

The Board of Directors of Marby Plastics plc is considering investing in new computer-controlled manufacturing machinery. The Directors have considered the following methods of financing the new machinery.

Retained Profit　　　　**Share Issue**　　　　**Bank Loan**

Recommend to the Directors, giving reasons, which method of finance you would choose and which you would reject. **(12)**

Student Answer

The Board of Directors of Marby Plastics has three options for financing the new machinery. The first option, Retained Profit, is only possible if the business has made a profit in previous years which it has not distributed to shareholders in the form of dividends. The main benefits of this source of finance is that no interest is payable as it is the company's own capital. A possible drawback of using this source of capital is that should the company need finance for any other purpose it will no longer be available. There is, therefore, an opportunity cost of using retained profit to fund the new equipment. Retained profit is an internal source of finance.

Share capital has the advantage of not needing to be paid back. However, selling shares may result in other people or organisations taking control of the business. Shareholders will also expect a return on their investment in the form of dividends. A bank loan, like share capital, is an external source of finance. A bank loan will have to repaid in full together with interest so this could possibly be an expensive source of finance if someone can be found who is prepared to lend the money.

In the light of this information, the best option for the company would probably be a combination of retained profit together with sale of a limited number of shares. This may help to overcome the disadvantages of each of these two options. A bank loan is probably the most costly of the three options.

Asif

What the Examiner Says

This is a very good answer. Asif has considered each option in turn and put forward some advantages and disadvantages. He has then gone on to make a recommendation, as required by the question. His solution is particularly interesting in that he has not put forward just one option but has suggested a combination. He has also given a justification for why he is recommending a combination. The only thing that he might have been able to add to his answer is that it can be costly to sell shares and there is no guarantee that sufficient shares will be purchased to finance the new investment.

This is a Level 3 (9 – 12 marks) answer
Marks awarded – 11 out of 12

Question Three (Common Question)

The following information is an extract from the Balance Sheets of Fiesta Manufacturing Ltd. Use the information to help answer some the questions which follow.

	2000	2001	2002
CURRENT ASSETS	£m	£m	£m
Stock	440	980	1 400
Debtors	400	480	470
Cash at Bank and in hand	110	48	10
CURRENT LIABILITIES			
Creditors	210	360	560
Overdraft	300	520	640
ACID TEST RATIO	1	0.6	0.4

a) Explain the difference between Current Assets and Current Liabilities. **(3)**
b) Explain why sufficient working capital is important to a business like Fiesta Manufacturing Ltd. **(4)**
c) Comment on the changes in Fiesta Manufacturing Ltd's liquidity position. **(6)**
d) Recommend, to the business, how it might improve its liquidity. **(8)**

Student Answer

a) The difference between current assets and current liabilities is that current assets are what the business owns and current liabilities are what the business owes.

b) Working capital = Current Assets minus Current Liabilities. Working capital is the money required for the day-to-day running of the business. If the business does not have sufficient Working Capital it may not be able to pay workers or buy replacement stock.

c) The Acid Test Ratio should preferably be between 0.8 and 1.0 in order for a business not to have liquidity problems. However, in 2001 and 2002 the Acid Test ratio dropped to a low figure. The business may therefore have a problem with its liquidity. The problem is due to a massive rise in creditors and overdraft, with only a small rise in debtors.

d) This business appears to have a liquidity problem. There has been a significant increase in the value of stock between 2000 and 2002. Too much cash may be tied up in this asset and the business should look for ways of reducing stock levels. The business should also look into ways of encouraging debtors to pay up more quickly for goods received. Whilst the amount has not increased there is still a lot of money owed to Fiesta Manufacturing Ltd. If this were to happen, it may allow the business to reduce the size of its overdraft which has been increasing steadily.

Rachel

What the Examiner Says

a) Rachel's answer is correct. However, she perhaps should have provided a little bit more detail by stating that current liabilities can be turned into cash quickly and current liabilities have to be repaid usually with one year.

Marks awarded – 2 out of 3

b) This is a good answer. A definition of the term has been given together with an accurate explanation, with examples, of what the term means and how a lack of working capital may affect a business.

Marks awarded – 4 out of 4

c) The question has not been answered fully. Rachel has correctly identified that the Acid Test ratio is a measure of liquidity which has an ideal answer which the company has failed to achieve in 2001 and 2002. An attempt has been made to identify the reasons for the problem. However, she should have gone on to calculate the Current Ratio for each year so that an even more detailed comment on the firm's liquidity position could have been made. Had she done so, she would have seen that this ratio was also falling **and** below an acceptable level of safety.

Marks awarded – 4 out of 6

d) Although a relatively short answer, a good attempt has been made at answering this question. Good answers do not always have to be long-winded! The information in the question has been carefully analysed and sound solutions have been put forward which will have a significant impact on the liquidity of the business if carried out. Reference, perhaps, should have been made to the Current and Acid Test Ratios.

This is a Level 3 (7–8 marks) answer
Marks awarded – 7 out of 8

Question Four (Higher Tier)

Christine and John McCormack think they have a good business idea. However, before they can start their business they need a loan. Their local bank manager has said that he is not able to help until they provide a Cash Flow Forecast for their business idea. Unfortunately, they are not sure what to do and have asked you for help.

a) Explain to Christine and John, the contents and purpose of a Cash Flow Forecast. **(6)**
b) Giving examples, explain how the bank manager might use the information in the Cash Flow Forecast to decide whether to grant Christine and John the loan they have asked for. **(8)**

Student Answer

a) *A cash flow forecast contains details of all the funds expected to flow into and out of the business in a certain period of time. This would include forecasts of sales income and the expenses which the business expects to have. This information then allows the business to work out when it may have a surplus or shortage of cash.*

b) *The bank manager will be able to use the information in the cash flow forecast to assess whether it is a good idea to lend the business money. Whilst the forecast does not calculate how much profit the business is likely to make it does show whether the business is likely to achieve sufficient sales income in relation to the costs of the running the business and whether the business is going to be able to afford to repay the loan. The forecast will help identify particular times when the business may be short of cash and when it may have a cash surplus. In addition to sales income, the forecast will also show other sources of income which Christine and John hope to have.*

James

What the Examiner Says

a) A relatively brief answer. James could, and should, have provided a little more detail by giving examples of different types of expenses which most businesses usually have. No reference has been made to the fact that the amount of the cash surplus or deficit at the end of one month is carried forward to the beginning of the next month. Mention should also have been made of the fact that one of the purposes of the cash flow forecast is to help the business plan ahead and manage its cash efficiently, by looking to see if it needs to try to increase sales or reduce costs at particular times.

This is a Level 1 (1–3 marks) response
Marks awarded – 3 out of 6

b) This is a good answer. James has considered how the bank manager will use the information in the forecast to help make a decision. Examples have been provided to illustrate the points James has made. James has quite correctly identified that the main concern of the bank manager is whether the business will be able to afford to repay the loan. The only thing which James might have been able to add is that the figures in the forecast are only estimates and that there is therefore no guarantee that the figures will be 100% accurate.

This is a Level 3 (7–8 marks) response
Marks awarded – 7 out of 8

Question Five (Common Question)
a) Explain the difference between:
   i)   Gross and Net profit.   **(4)**
   ii) Profit and Cash flow.   **(4)**
b) Making a Profit is important for most businesses.
   Explain why this is the case.   **(8)**

Student Answer

a) i) Gross profit is sales revenue less the cost of goods sold. Net Profit is Gross Profit less expenses. Net profit is the amount of profit left over once the expenses of running the business have been deducted from the Gross Profit.

ii) Profit is the amount of money left over after a business has paid for all the costs of running the business. Cash Flow, on the other hand, is the flow of money into and out of the business over a particular period of time.

b) It is important for a business to make a profit because it is necessary for the business to expand. Without profit, the business would not be able to pay for new equipment. Shareholders will also want the business to make a profit because they will want some of this profit in the form of dividends. If the business does not a make a profit the possibility exists that the business may become insolvent. Profit will allow the business to compete in a market and take advantage of any upturns in the economy.

Laura

What the Examiner Says

a) i)   This a good answer both types of profit have been correctly defined to help distinguish between them.
Marks awarded – 4 out of 4

ii) Another good answer. Clear definitions have been provided which distinguish between the two terms.
Marks awarded – 4 out of 4

b) This answer is not as clear as it could have been. There are some relevant statements which are in need of a little more detail and explanation. Laura has included some relevant facts but they are not very clearly explained. There are also some inaccurate statements. It would have been much better had she explained, first, that without a making a profit it would be unlikely that the business would be able to pay its running costs. If this were to be the case, it is highly likely that the business would fail and become insolvent. She has correctly identified that profit is a major source of internal finance for most businesses and that, in Limited companies, there is an expectation by shareholders that they will receive a dividend, in return for investing in the business, based on the profit made. The final statement regarding being able to compete in the economy is irrelevant.

This is a Level 2 (4 – 6 marks) answer
Marks awarded – 5 out of 8

Marketing

SECTION 4

SOME BASICS

Marketing is **not** just about selling a product or a service. It is the ways in which a business identifies the needs of its customers, produces goods or services that customers want, informs customers about its products or services through advertising and promotions, sets a price that customers will pay, makes sure that the products or services are available when and where customers want, and finally makes sure the customer is satisfied with the level of service given or quality of product received.

When **all** of the above are working well **together**, the business has a successful marketing strategy. Although you will learn the different parts of marketing separately, you need to understand how the different parts outlined above affect each other.

Revision Material

KNOWLEDGE HIERARCHY: MARKETING

This information is intended to provide a quick reminder. Your notes, and the information in the textbook you have used, should provide more detailed information and examples.

Analysing the Market

Topic	Key Features	Detail	Further Information
Market Orientation	• Aimed at consumer	• Used by most businesses	• More sure of success • More costly
Product Orientation	• Producing what business wants	• Used in the past, little used now	• May lead to expensive failures • Avoids cost of market research
Market Segments	• Splits up the market	• Age, gender quality, etc. • Socio-economic Groups	• A, B, C1, C2, D and E or Groups 1 to 5
Identify Disposable Income	• Money left after paying essential bills	• Important for more luxury products and services	
Mass Market	• Aimed at most consumers	• E.g. Ford cars	
Niche Market	• Aimed at a smaller market	• E.g. Ferrari cars	
Test Market	• Marketing in a restricted area	• Helps business trial products before selling to full market	• May save time and money
Market Research – Primary	• Sometimes called field research	• Questionnaires, interviews • Sampling	• Provides detailed accurate information on products • More costly • Quota, random
Primary	• Consumer panels	• Groups used to reporting on products	• Used by larger businesses
Primary	• Testing/observing	• Used in developing food/drink products	• Unsuitable for many products
Market Research – Secondary	• Can be called desk research	• Census, Internet, internal data, trade information	• Cheaper • May not accurately meet business needs
SWOT analysis	• Strengths Weaknesses Opportunities Threats	• Used for new product/activity	• Useful when comparing performance with other businesses
USP analysis	• Unique selling point	• Identifies differences in product/service	• Used in promotions to market the product

The Market Mix

Topic	Key Features	Detail	Further Information
Product	• Product mix/range	• Types of product/ service offered	• May be a budget range and an up-market range
	• Customer needs	• Design	• Size, colour, appeal
	• Branding	• Developing a known name	• E.g. Kellogg's, Sony, Nike, Cadbury
	• Research and development	• Changes to existing products or developing new ones	• Leads to product innovation, e.g. Dyson cleaners
	• Product life cycle	• Introduction Growth Maturity Saturation Decline	• Stages of life cycle affect other parts of market mix
	• Extension strategies	• Adding value, price reduction, re-launch	• Used when product is at maturity stage
Price	• Competition based	• Higher, lower, the same	• Important for new businesses or new products • Higher indicates exclusive, etc.
	• Penetration	• Lower price then higher	• Used to gain market share
	• Skimming/creaming	• Higher price for time when product is new	• Used in high tech products, e.g. games consoles
	• Cost Plus	• Costs plus profit	• Essential if losses to be avoided
	• Differential	• Different prices for same product or service	• Often used in transport
	• Promotional	• Price reduction for short time	• E.g. the January sales
	• Psychological	• £99.99 rather than £100	• Widely used for all types of products
	• Supply	• The business side of marketing	• Amount a business is prepared to sell • Businesses want higher prices
	• Demand	• The consumer side of marketing	• Amount consumers are prepared to buy • Consumers want lower prices

Topic	Key Features	Detail	Further Information
Price *cont.*	• Elasticity	• How demand changes when price changes • Can affect marketing strategies and promotional activities	• Measured in % • Important when considering a change in price
Place	• Direct	• Internet, mail order	• Used by smaller businesses • Not suitable for all products
	• Through retailer or wholesaler	• Shops, catalogues, markets	• Most goods sold this way, e.g. food, clothes, cars
Promotion	• Advertising	• Persuasive, informative	• Persuasive, gives opinions • Informative, gives facts
	• Media	• Television, radio, newspapers, magazines, Internet, billboards, cinema	• Choice depends on cost, type of product, target market to be reached
	• Sales promotions	• BOGOF, added value, loss leader, competitions, free sample, merchandising, guarantees	• Choice depends on product, stage of life cycle, target market
	• Public relations (PR)	• Keeping business in the public eye	• E.g. newspaper stories, magazine articles rather than adverts
	• Sponsorship	• Often used in sport	• E. g. Barclaycard, Nationwide, Embassy, N Power, Zurich

Consumer Protection

Topic	Key Features	Detail	Further information
The Law	• Supply of Goods Act	• Goods are satisfactory quality, as described, fit for purpose	• Money back for consumer if law broken
	• Weights and Measures Act	• Certain products only	• E.g. alcohol sold in certain measures • Enforced by Trading Standards
	• Consumer Protection Acts	• Labelling of dangerous products • Laws on the advertising of sale prices	• Identifies rights of consumers and responsibilities of retailers • Sold for 28 days at previous price
	• Food and Drugs Acts	• Labelling of food, and contents • Who can buy/sell drugs	• E.g. orange juice, orange squash must have certain orange content
	• Consumer Credit Act	• APR must be stated • Credit agreement given to consumer	• Consumer can compare credit terms
	• European Union	• Directives given on food and doorstop selling amongst others	• E.g. colouring allowed in food
Trade organisations	• E.g. Association of British Travel Agents (ABTA)	• Membership is voluntary • Gives consumer confidence	• Compensation if a problem with holiday
Independent organisations	• Consumer's Association • Citizens Advice Bureau	• Produce Which? Magazine	• Independent comparison of products
Government organisations	• 'Watchdogs' • Office of Fair Trading	• OFTEL, OFWAT are examples • Influences mergers and takeovers	• Control prices • Influence marketing activity • Investigates if mergers, etc. are in the interests of the consumer

PUTTING IT IN CONTEXT

Matt Richards Ltd is a company which makes designer plastic products such as waste-paper bins, pen holders and letter racks. It is a *market orientated* business, always making sure that consumers like a new product before it is developed fully. The managing director of the company, Matt, believes this approach will save the company money, even though it will mean some *market research* has to be carried out.

The market for the company's product is a *niche* one. Matt knows that he is aiming the products at a small market. He feels the business is not big enough to supply goods to a larger *mass market*. The target market for the designer products are 20- to 30-year olds in *socio-economic groups* A, B, and C1 who are prepared to spend rather more money on items for the home that are a little different. These groups, being more wealthy, have a greater *disposable income* to spend on such items.

Matt is now developing a new range of products for the kitchen. His designers have come up with new ideas for food containers and general storage. Matt knows that the next stage will need some detailed *market research*. He decides to ask a business specialising in market research to carry out some *primary research*, conducting *interviews* with the *target market*. The *sample* of people asked is chosen by the *quota* method, as information is only really needed from the top range (A, B and C1) of the *socio-economic* groups.

When a new product range is developed, the company takes the opportunity to conduct a *SWOT* analysis in order to examine their strengths, weaknesses opportunities and threats in relation to the new products. Matt knows that the main *strength* of the business is their unique designs, but recognises that the price is high and this is seen as a *weakness*. There are other businesses which make plastic kitchen containers which is clearly a *threat*, but there are great *opportunities* with the growth in sales of specialist kitchen equipment in recent years. Overall the *USP* (Unique Selling Point) of the business is thought to be the design, and it is thought that this should be the main theme of any future *advertising* for the new products.

When the products were being developed, Matt held a meeting to decide on how the kitchen products should be marketed. The meeting decided to use the *market mix* as a framework for discussion. The business knows that for a successful *marketing strategy*, all parts of the market mix should work together.

There would be a *product mix* of different colours and sizes of containers. The *product life cycle* was thought to be about two years before new designs would be needed.

The *price* would be *competitor*-based, but a little higher to indicate better quality. At first there may be a *promotional pricing* period to introduce the new range. The accountant pointed out that any costs of production, development and marketing must be recovered in the final price, and so cost *plus* pricing should not be ignored.

Success in marketing requires the correct mix

The *advertising* of the product would be in specialist *trade magazines* for the shops who bought the products, and in up-market newspapers with a high A, B and C1 readership. Giving some containers as prizes in television cooking shows was thought to be a good *PR* exercise.

The *place* where the products were sold was discussed at the meeting. The present *method of distribution* was to sell to up-market high street shops, but the marketing manager, Heather, was keen to go into *direct marketing*, selling the new kitchen containers on the *Internet*, and by *mail order*. Heather thought that this would increase profit, as it would cut out the shops. As the products were aimed at more wealthy consumers they would most likely have a computer at home through which to order.

When the marketing material was being put together, the company had to be careful to describe the products accurately; otherwise it would be breaking the *Sale of Goods Act*. Matt also checked to see if any *directives* from the *European Union* affected the manufacture and sale of plastic food containers. He, too, didn't want to break any laws!

ACTIVITIES

ACTIVITY ONE

Design a questionnaire to find out consumer opinions on a new range of hair shampoo. You should include questions on:

- Price
- Place
- Possible Promotions
- Products
- Any other areas you feel may provide useful information

Your questionnaire must have *at least* 10 questions.

Explain how you will a) identify your sample, b) carry out the questionnaire.

ACTIVITIES *cont.*

Look at another questionnaire designed by a friend. Explain how you might have been able to improve it.

Remember, in a questionnaire you should be aiming to collect information that will enable a business to develop a successful marketing strategy.

ACTIVITY TWO

What *pricing* strategy would be suitable for the following situations? Give reasons for your answer.

Setting the correct price for a product is a complicated process

- A little-known electrical business wants to enter the widescreen television market.
- A famous chocolate maker has developed a new caramel-flavoured snack.
- A car maker has an old model car coming towards the end of its product life cycle.
- A well-known computer games console maker introduces a new revolutionary product, more powerful than any of its competitors.
- An established airline business wants to increase sales. The business has a lot of competitors.

ACTIVITY THREE

1. Complete the following spider diagram to show the methods of promotion that might be used by a national fast-food chain.

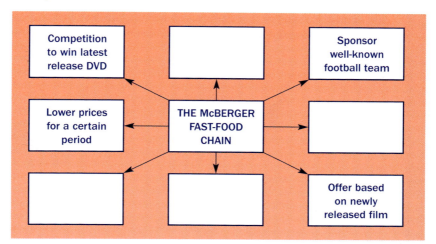

2. Explain why the methods of promotion would be suitable for a national fast food restaurant
3. Complete a similar spider diagram and explanation for Leopard, a car manufacturer wanting to introduce a new, fast sports car

ACTIVITY FOUR

Plan a marketing strategy for a well known drinks company wanting to introduce a new fruit-flavoured soft drink. You have the following further information:

- The target market is 10- to 25-year olds, male and female
- The makers want to emphasise the health qualities of the drink
- A large marketing budget is available

In completing the strategy, **all** aspects of the marketing mix should be covered, emphasising how **each** of the four Ps of the marketing mix work **together** to produce a successful strategy. Your marketing strategy should be between one and two sides of A4 paper.

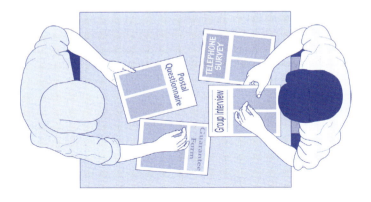

Questions that ask you to give the meaning and examples of terms such as:

- *Primary and Secondary Research*
- *Market Segments*
- *SWOT and USP Analysis*
- *The Four Ps of the Market Mix*
- *The Stages of the Product Life Cycle*
- *Skimming, Penetration and other pricing strategies*
- *Direct Marketing*
- *Point of Sale, Loss Leaders and other methods of sales promotion*
- *Consumer Protection*

More difficult questions you may be asked:

- *Explain the suitability of using primary research for a particular situation.*
- *Evaluate the benefits of using SWOT analysis in a particular situation.*
- *Explain how the market mix may be applied to different products and services.*
- *Evaluate the use of different parts of the market mix at different stages of the product life cycle.*
- *Explain how a business might develop a marketing strategy for a particular product*
- *Analyse the way in which different promotion techniques are used in different stages of the product life cycle.*
- *Evaluate the use of Internet-based marketing compared to more traditional High Street stores.*
- *Explain how and why consumers are protected by law.*
- *Explain how a business might benefit from using different pricing strategies.*

Some examples of these types of questions are given in the following section. Look carefully at what the question is asking you to do; how the student has answered the question; what the examiner thinks of the answer

MARKETING: SPECIMEN QUESTIONS

Question one (Common Question)

a) Explain what is meant by the following pricing strategies:
   i) Skimming
   ii) Penetration **(4)**
b) Explain **two** promotion methods a business might use to increase sales. **(4)**

Student Answer

a) Skimming is where a new product is priced very highly to entice the wealthy buyers to buy on the assumption that as it is very expensive and new then the product must be of a very good quality and be worth buying. It can also be said to have a 'prestige' value meaning that it is better than anything else – very high class/quality.

Penetration pricing is where a company will set a very low price for their product in order to attract a large number of customers and hence increase its market share very quickly as its competitors charge a much higher price for relatively the same product.

b) *A business could increase its sales by advertising the product in question either on TV or radio, or any other forms of media, for that matter. This would increase the number of people that actually know the product exists and if the product is made desirable, whether by its appearance or price, then the potential customer would be enticed into buying the product. Also, as another form of increasing sales, a business could offer free testing of the product, be it a free trial for an Internet supplier or a free sample of a piece of shortbread. This would have the same affect as advertising as it would increase the number of people wanting to buy the product.*

Sarah

What the Examiner Says

a) Sarah has answered this very well, up to a point. She clearly understands that skimming will mean a higher price, which may well mean that a product has a high prestige value. What she has failed to recognise is that skimming has a time span, and that in time the higher price will be reduced as new products come along.

With penetration pricing the same mistake has been made. Yes, the price will be lower to attract customers, but this will increase over time as customers become aware of the brand and product.

Marks awarded – 2 out of 4

b) Sarah has answered this section very well. She has concentrated on two distinct promotion activities, advertising and free trials. These are clearly explained with relevant examples.

Marks awarded – 4 out of 4

Question Two (Higher Tier)

Emotions Ltd makes skincare products.
They concentrate on the teenage market, both boys and girls, and have a new product aimed at the prevention of teenage spots. Recommend a marketing strategy Emotions Ltd might use for this new product. **(12)**

Student Answer

For teenagers it is always worthwhile advertising on TV as that is what most of them watch on a daily basis, also the time is important of the screening of the advert – it needs to be in between a teenage programme – not many teenagers are caught watching 'Countdown'! Also you have to prove that it does work by testing it in the first place and labelling it as dermatologically tested. If you would want them to believe you more you could employ a famous personality that is respected by both sexes, for instance by having David Beckham say that it does work.

Also you would need to make the product desirable, not many teenagers talk about what skincare products they use so it is important not to rely on knowledge of the product being passed around by word-of-mouth and the company would have to count on designing a product that would be sufficiently eye-catching and grab the teenager's attention so that they actually feel like buying it.

Finally, price can be important due to the low budget of a teenager. However, it may be possible that they can just ask their parents to buy it next time they do the weekly family shop. Another idea for the teenagers is offering a free trial-period pack where they can have a free pack that would last them for, let's say, two weeks and if they don't notice a difference then they haven't lost any money. However if the product does work and reduces their spots then they may feel more confident in buying it, as they know for a fact without spending anything that it will work on their face. This would cause profits to be slack at first, but if the product did work then profits should increase dramatically.

Damon

What the Examiner Says

With any question asking for a marketing strategy, the market mix can be used as a framework, but it is *vital* that the answer shows how the market mix works *together* to produce a successful strategy.

Damon has identified advertising, trial packs and endorsement (David Beckham) as part of promotion. Price is seen as an issue, as is the design of the product itself. There is no clear reference to place, i.e. where the product is to be sold and the distribution methods to be used.

Damon has chosen his examples well, indicating where and when the product should be advertised, and the endorsement link is well made. The reference to testing is important in the modern marketplace. The section on price could have been covered in more business-like terms, for example should the business use penetration or skimming methods?

What the answer lacks is how the elements of the market mix will work together. For example the advertising should emphasise the pricing strategy, which will display the characteristics of the product, with a clear distribution plan to ensure that the product is available in outlets that the target market will use (or their parents, as identified by Damon!).

Question Three (Higher Tier)

Quench is a new soft drink made by Fisher Ltd. Quench is to be targeted at adult consumers wanting to keep fit and enjoy a refreshing drink.

Evaluate the different advertising media Fisher Ltd might use for Quench.

(8)

Student Answer

If you want to target a specific audience then Fisher Ltd would need to find out what that specific audience either listens to, reads or watches so that they know where to advertise their new product. It may be that they have to advertise in fitness magazines to attract that particular niche market. Also a good idea would be to have the new drink, Quench, on sale in places that fitness people go to, such as gyms, knowing that they would be thirsty after a good workout and they would have this new drink at hand ready to be bought. If the price is sufficiently tempting it would be highly likely that they would go for Quench over another well-known invigorating drink.

Tracy

What the Examininer Says

Tracy starts her answer well, explaining that Fisher Ltd would certainly have to conduct their own research into their target market. Having said that she chooses an example well, in fitness magazines. The answer then begins to fall away. Whilst the sale of the drink in gyms would also advertise the product, sales and advertising should be separated when answering the question. The reference to price is not required.

The vital element which Tracy has missed is that the command word is '*evaluate*'. This means that she should have examined the different *media* (not the place of sale as such) which Fisher Ltd might use and then judge, giving reasons, which is the most appropriate, in her opinion, for the new soft drink. For example other media include TV, newspapers, cinemas, radio, etc. A number of these could have formed the basis for the evaluation of the most appropriate media for Fisher Ltd to use.

Coldstream plc make washing machines. At present they only sell to main electrical shops who then sell on to consumers. The marketing manager now feels that they should sell direct to the consumer.

Evaluate the different methods of direct sales, recommending to Coldstream whether they should change to this new method of distribution. **(10)**

Student Answer

If Coldstream wanted to sell direct to the consumer they would have to consider many factors such as marketing their product by themselves, as they sell direct to retailers who normally know what they're doing – if they offer a quality product that is reasonably priced, chances are they would buy your product.

However due to Coldstream wanting to take the retailer out of the equation then they would have to advertise direct to the consumer and in that spend a lot more on advertising. Also profits would reduce in the short term because of the extra costs of advertising a new service. Further costs would come from the setting up of a distribution section and customer service, as the shops would no longer play this role. Consumers will need to see the benefits of direct sales, rather than buying at places such as Currys.

Coldstream also have many other options available to them if they did decide to go ahead with the plan. For instance they could go for mail order instead of opening a shop themselves – this would basically be a consumer ordering direct from the factory. Or Coldstream could go for a factory shop instead of different shops scattered around the country.

A further option would be to sell on the Internet. The company (being a plc) would have a website already and so the extra cost of setting up a sales page would be minimal

My opinion is that Coldstream should make a compromise at first and operate an Internet system that would stretch out to the entire country (at minimal cost) while at the same time having a shop in the factories. If this is found to be a success then they may choose to expand further and open separate shops themselves around the country, and set up a mail order business. There will be costs in the short term for the new service but in the long run I feel that the direct sales will work, providing the product is good and the price is attractive to consumers.

Ben

What the Examiner Says

This question falls into two parts, the evaluation of direct sales methods, and whether direct selling should be adopted by Coldstream plc.

Ben covers both parts well. He identifies various direct selling methods (Internet, mail order, factory shops) and recognises that costs will be involved with them all, though the Internet approach is favoured as the addition to an existing website will keep costs down.

Problems associated with direct selling are dealt with very well. The cost of setting up such a system, including advertising, customer services, etc. are covered in some detail.

The judgement at the end of the answer is well made, looking at a gradual approach to the change, whist recognising that there must be a quality product at an attractive price to tempt consumers away from more traditional outlets such as Currys.

This is a top Level 3 (8–10 marks) answer, with Ben being awarded full marks

Question Five (Common Question)

a) Explain how government 'watchdogs' such as OFTEL help protect the consumer **(4)**

b) Explain **two** other ways in which the consumer is protected when buying goods and services. **(4)**

Student Answer

a)   OFTEL is responsible for the phone industry, be it the mobile phone industry or cable or privatised phones. OFTEL is always regulating the prices of calls and ensuring that the customer is fairly treated.

b) A consumer can usually take a product back, if he/she still has the receipt for the product. This may be because they are not happy with the product or that there is something wrong with the product itself. Also a customer is protected by the Office of Fair Trading in general, which ensures that the consumer is not treated in an offensive way and is given a fair deal for a product and not 'ripped off'.

Kirsty

Production

SECTION 5

SOME BASICS

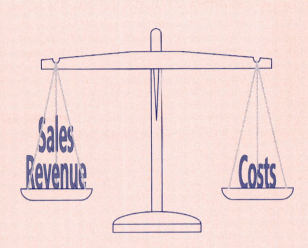

A firm breaks even when sales revenue equal costs

All businesses must carefully monitor their costs, both variable and fixed. Costs should always be less than revenue in the long term in order to provide a profit. Where total costs equal total revenue, a business is said to break even. The calculation of break-even is useful for a business in order that it knows the number of products it needs to sell, or the value of services it needs to provide, before it makes a profit. The calculation itself, however, may not always be useful for a business.

A business may grow in many ways, by integrating with other businesses or simply growing by itself. The growth of a business may bring benefits such as economies of scale, and an ability to change the method of production it has used. Quality and productivity are essential if a business is to remain competitive.

Revision Material

This information is intended to provide a quick reminder. Your notes, and the information in the textbook you have used, should provide more detailed information and examples.

Costs, Revenue and Break-Even

Topic	Key Features	Detail	Further Information
Costs	• Fixed costs	• Do not change with level of production	• E.g. Rent, Business Rates
	• Variable costs	• Change with level of production	• E.g. Materials
	• Total costs	• Fixed costs plus variable costs	
	• Average costs	• Total costs divided by number sold	• Helps to set price
Revenues	• Sales revenue	• Quantity sold multiplied by selling price	• Often called sales turnover
Break-Even	• Where total costs equal total revenue	• No profit or loss is made	
	• Contribution	• Selling price minus variable cost per unit	
	• Formula for calculation of break-even	• Total fixed costs divided by contribution	• May be used to decide on price levels
	• Margin of safety	• The amount by which sales are more than the break-even level	• Often confused with profit
	• Limitations of use	• All forecasts are liable to change	• Costs of business might change
		• Assumption that all production is sold	
		• Activities of competitors might change	• Competitors may lower their prices
	• Benefits of use	• Helps plan ahead • Production levels and market price can be identified • Often a minimum aim of a business	• Often used when business is new or launching a new product

Types and Scale of Production

Topic	Key Features	Detail	Further Information
Scale of Production	• Capacity of a business	• Above capacity	• Producing more than the resources should be capable of doing
		• Below capacity	• Producing less than the business should be capable of doing
Business Growth	• Economies of scale	• Unit cost reduced as production increases	
		• Purchasing	• Discount for buying goods in bulk
		• Managerial	• Specialist managers improve performance
		• Financial	• Cost of raising finance is less
		• Marketing	• Savings on advertising and distribution
		• Risk bearing	• Firm not dependent on one product
		• Technical	• Firm can buy the most efficient machinery
	• Diseconomies of scale	• Unit costs increase as production increases	• Problems with communication and control
Integration	• Merger	• Two or more firms agree to join	• Can be agreed or hostile where no agreement
	• Takeover	• A firm buying the control of another	• May be subject to government approval
	• Internal growth	• A firm growing on its own	
	• Vertical	• Forwards vertical	• E.g. Furniture maker takes over furniture shop
		• Backwards vertical	• E.g. Furniture maker takes over wood supplier
	• Horizontal	• A firm joining with another firm involved in the same business	• Furniture maker joins with another furniture maker

Topic	Key Features	Detail	Further Information
Integration *cont.*	• Diversification	• A firm joining with another firm in a different business	• Furniture maker joins with travel business
Measuring Business Size	• Sales	• The total value of goods sold	• May be a small firm but selling high cost items, e.g. jewellery
	• Market share	• The % of a total market a firm controls	• Often used in car industry
	• Number of employees	• Can be a problem with capital intensive firms	
Methods of Production	• Job	• Each product individually produced	• E.g. Handmade furniture
	• Batch	• A number of products made at the same time	• E.g. Loaves of bread
	• Flow	• Made on an assembly line	• E.g. Cars. Work often repetitive
Division of Labour	• Each worker concentrates on one job	• Less training • Quicker completion • More efficient use of time • Can lead to boredom	• Often used in flow production • Lack of motivation if work is very repetitive
Technology and Production	• CAD	• Computer aided design	• Saves time and expensive testing
	• CAM	• Computer aided manufacture	• Less labour needed. Saves costs in long term
	• CIM	• Computer integrated manufacture	• All the business is computer controlled

Productivity and Quality Control

Topic	Key Features	Detail	Further Information
Productivity	• Producing more per worker	• Involves greater flexibility from workers	• Can lead to problems between management and workers
	• Lean production	• Cutting down on all production costs • Includes JIT (Just In Time) methods	• Reduces stock • Saves storage costs
Quality Control	• May be a separate department		
	• Total Quality Management (TQM)	• All workers involved	• Workers responsible for quality of their own work

PUTTING IT IN CONTEXT

Tim and Mel are partners trading as Devilish Stagewear. Tim has experience as a keyboard player in a band and his partner Mel was a seamstress making clothing for a number of years. They feel there is a market for specialist stagewear aimed at the growing number of amateur and professional bands.

Both Tim and Mel are aware of their *costs*. As they operate from home they hope to minimise their *fixed costs* such as *rent* and *business rates*, though the expensive *material* costs for the stagewear will make up a large proportion of their *variable costs*. *Revenue* will come from the sales of the outfits Mel produces, which in the first six months of the business were above the *break-even* figure required. Projected sales for the next six months are higher, taking the business further into the *margin of safety*.

The partners are aware that their calculations, such as *break-even*, may not always be accurate. Tim wonders whether other businesses may start with the same ideas on making stagewear and possibly take some of their custom. Mel is more concerned at the price of the material she has to buy, as she knows that a future price rise will severely affect their calculations. There is no real scope for *computer aided manufacture*, the business is too small, though Mel sees *computer aided design* as a help to produce eye catching stagewear.

Producing *quality* goods is vital for Tim and Mel if they are to gain a good reputation and secure further orders. They plan to operate on a *Total Quality Management* approach, with each worker being responsible for the quality of their own work. Tim is responsible for the quality of the administration and sales service, Mel being responsible for the quality of the stagewear she makes. The partnership will operate their own *Just-In-Time* method of production, with materials arriving only when needed. This will save the business *costs* of holding expensive *stock* of specialist material.

The partners hope that the business will grow in the future, and so be able to take advantage of *economies of scale*. Mel will be able to buy the material she needs in *bulk*, and more advanced sewing machinery to speed up manufacture. This will help reduce the costs of the business. Any future growth is expected to be *internal* (there are no other businesses concentrating on stagewear), though there is the possibility of some *diversification* if Tim develops his electrical experience and produces electrical safety equipment for bands and clubs.

 # ACTIVITIES

ACTIVITY ONE

Sarah Langley owns Floral Art, specialising in quality flower arrangements. Below is a list of some of her costs:

- Rent
- Business Rates
- Flowers for the arrangements
- Bank loan
- An advertisement every week in the local paper
- Ribbons for the arrangements
- Business cards
- Postage

Put each of the costs into the correct column in your own copy of the chart similar to the one below.

Fixed Costs	Variable Costs

ACTIVITY TWO

The following are definitions of terms used in connection with break-even. What is the name of the term to which each definition refers?

a) The difference between the break-even level of output and a higher level of output at which a profit is made.
b) Selling price minus the variable costs per unit.
c) Where total costs equal total revenue.
d) Costs which rise and fall with the level of production.
e) The money received from sales.
f) Costs which remain the same when the level of production changes.

Draw a break-even chart and show each of the terms in the correct position on the chart.

ACTIVITY THREE

Nazish and Rachael want to start a business making picture frames. They have identified the following costs for their business.

Cost	Amount
Rent and Business Rates	£100 per week
Materials per frame	£2.50
Other variable costs per frame	£3.50

They expect to sell each frame for £10.

a) Calculate the number of frames that Nazish and Sarah must sell per week in order to break even.

b) Draw a break-even chart to show the break-even position of the business.

c) Using the break-even chart, or further calculations, show how the break-even amount would change if the price they charged per frame was:
   i)   Increased to £16
   ii) Decreased to £8

ACTIVITY FOUR

Below are features connected with the growth of businesses. Expand the diagram below as far as you can to explain how each feature affects business activity. A start has been made for you (for example there are more economies of scale, etc.). Look to show what each box can lead to. Use a LARGE piece of paper!

ACTIVITIES *cont.*

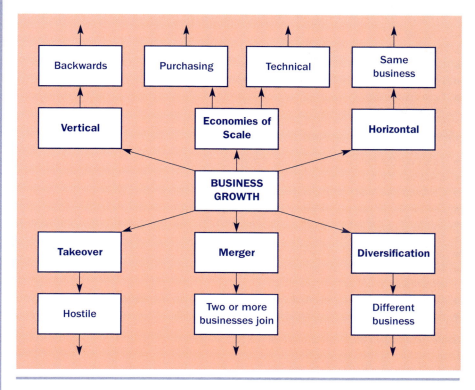

Backwards	Purchasing	Technical	Same business
Vertical	Economies of Scale		Horizontal
	BUSINESS GROWTH		
Takeover	Merger		Diversification
Hostile	Two or more businesses join		Different business

ACTIVITY FIVE

From your local area, find examples of businesses which use the following methods of production:

- Job
- Batch
- Flow

For **each** business, explain:

a) How the production method works in practice.
b) Why the production method is suited to the business, stating the advantages and disadvantages of this method over the production methods not used.

QUESTION TYPES TO EXPECT

Questions that ask you to give the meaning and examples of such terms as:

- *Fixed and Variable costs*
- *Break-even*

Production

- *Economies of Scale*
- *Diseconomies of Scale*
- *Integration: Vertical, Horizontal, Diversification*
- *Merger*
- *Takeover*
- *Job, Batch and Flow Production*
- *CAD, CAM and CIM*
- *Productivity*
- *Lean Production*
- *Total Quality Management*

More difficult questions you may be asked:

- *Calculate the total and average costs from figures provided.*
- *Calculate the break-even using a formula.*
- *Calculate the break-even using data from a table of figures provided.*
- *Draw and interpret a break-even graph to analyse the position of a business.*
- *Explain how a break-even calculation may be either useful or misleading for a business.*
- *Evaluate the economies of scale that may benefit a business in given circumstances.*
- *Analyse and evaluate the different methods of production available to a business.*
- *Identify and evaluate the benefits and problems associated with business growth through integration.*
- *Evaluate the benefits and problems of introducing improved technology within a business.*
- *Analyse and evaluate the benefits of a quality control system in a business.*

Some examples of these types of questions and student answers are given in the following section. Look carefully at what the question is asking you to do; how the student has answered the question; what the examiner thinks of the answer

PRODUCTION: SPECIMEN QUESTIONS

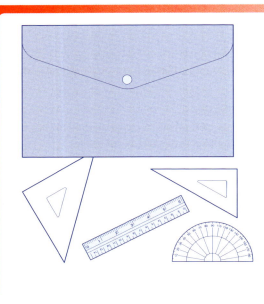

Question One (Higher Tier)

Bendit Ltd makes plastic rulers and other plastic stationery equipment. The weekly production costs for rulers are as follows:

Item	Cost
Plastic per ruler	2p
Other variable costs per ruler	3p
Rent	£250
Business Rates	£125

Bendit Ltd sells the rulers for 55p.

a) Using the data above, calculate the number of rulers Bendit Ltd must sell per week to break even. Show your working. **(4)**

b) Evaluate the benefits and problems of using break-even analysis for a business such as Bendit Ltd. **(8)**

Student Answer

a) $\text{Break-even} = \dfrac{\text{Fixed costs}}{\text{Selling price} - \text{Variable costs}}$

$= \dfrac{£250 + £175}{55p - (2p + 3p)}$

$= \dfrac{£425}{50p}$

$= 850 \text{ rulers per week to break even}$

b) Break-even is useful for a business because the business can plan ahead. It can plan the production levels necessary not only to break even but also move into the margin of safety and so be more certain of making a profit. Break-even also enables the business to see the effect of different prices for its products on the production levels to break even. The higher the price the fewer products need to be sold to break even.

The problems with break-even are that the business does not know if costs will change in the future. This will affect the break-even amount. Also competitors may change their prices, taking custom from the business and so affecting the break-even calculation.

Chris

What the Examiner Says

a) This is a very well set out answer. It is easy to follow how Chris has worked and it is accurate. Even if Chris had made a mistake in his final calculation he would have still been awarded some marks because of his understanding of which figures to use.

Marks awarded – 4 out of 4

b) Chris has explained very well the benefits and problems of using break-even. What he has not done is *evaluated* the benefits and problems. For example do the benefits make it worthwhile for a business to calculate breakeven, given the fact that there are problems? Or are the problems so great that completing a break-even calculation is a waste of time?

Chris might have achieved a Level 1 (1 – 4 marks) answer worth 4 out of the 8 marks available. Evaluation would have been necessary to achieve a Level 2 (5–8 marks) answer

Question Two (Common Question) Q

Longden Ltd prints books and magazines. It is considering taking over a competitor business Cropley Ltd, which also print books and magazines.

a) What type of integration is the proposed takeover of Cropley Ltd by Longden Ltd? **(1)**

b) Explain the benefits of this type of integration to Longden Ltd. **(6)**

Student Answer

a) This type of integration is called horizontal.

b) The benefits of this type of integration is that the business will be much bigger, which will make it much better. It can buy things in bulk which is much better than if you only bought a small amount. If you only bought a small amount then it will cost a lot more than if you bought a large amount, so this will be much better for Longden Ltd.

Sam

What the Examiner Says

a) Sam has correctly identified the takeover as being horizontal.

Marks awarded – 1 out of 1

b) In this section Sam seems to lose her way. She says little which is wrong, correctly identifying that the larger business will indeed be able to buy products at a lower price. This is really where her answer stops. She could have developed her answer to say that the lower price for paper and ink (it is a printing business) will help the business by reducing costs and so increase profits. This is only part of economies of scale. Other parts include technical, managerial and financial benefits (see Knowledge Hierarchy). Sam could also have explained how taking over a competitor business will give Longden Ltd a larger market share, and possibly be able to increase prices which again will help profits.

Marks awarded – 1 out of 6

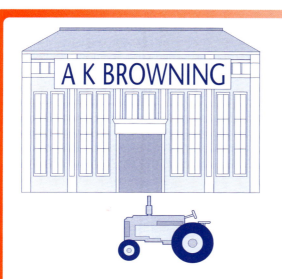

AK Browning plc make tractors. The tractors are finally assembled on a production line, using flow method of production. Many of the different parts used on each tractor are made by batch methods of production.

Evaluate the benefits of using different methods of production for the final assembly of the tractors and the making of the different parts. **(10)**

Student Answer

Making tractors is like making cars. They will move down on a conveyor belt and parts will be added to others to make the tractor. This is flow production. It is better than job and batch because:

- *It saves training workers and the costs involved. Each job is simple and repetitive. Job production means specialist workers who are highly trained (and so expensive to employ)*
- *A large amount can be made. Making an individual tractor (Job) will be slower and more expensive.*
- *Better use can be made of modern production methods such as robots and other computer controlled machinery. With job and batch production some machinery would be left idle for periods of time.*

Batch production is better for the tractor parts because:

- *The parts will be identical. They can be made by setting up a machine to make the number required. The machine settings will then be changed to make, for example, a different sized part. This saves time and money for the business.*
- *Job production is no good for the parts because job means creating a unique product. The parts are not unique*
- *Flow is no real use for the parts as you wouldn't have a nut and bolt being made on a production line.*

Steve

What the Examiner Says

Steve has recognised that the command word is *evaluate*. This means making a judgement on the situation you are given in the question. Here the question is asking you to evaluate the advantages of using different methods of production for the tractor assembly and the parts used to build the tractor.

Steve has done this well. He has not only looked at the advantages of using flow and batch production *for a tractor assembly* but he has also explained why other methods of production *would be less suitable*. It is this second point that is often missed in this type of question which asks you to evaluate.

This is a Level 3 (8–10 marks) answer
Marks awarded – 10

Question 4 (Common Question)

AJ Computers Ltd make computers for sale by mail order direct to the public. The business uses Total Quality Management throughout its operations.

a) Explain what is meant by Total Quality Management. **(2)**
b) Analyse the problems and benefits of introducing a Total Quality Management system into a business such as AJ Computers Ltd. **(6)**

Student Answer

a) Total Quality Management is when a business puts great importance on quality and everything is checked to make sure it is of the correct quality.
b) The problems of introducing Total Quality Management is that people have to do more work to check the quality and they might not want the extra work. The benefits are that with better quality more people will buy the computers.

Kevin

What the Examiner Says

a) Here Kevin has recognised that quality will be checked throughout the business (1 mark) but he has failed to say that in Total Quality Management *each* worker is responsible for the quality of their *own* work.

Marks awarded – 1 out of 2

b) The problem of workers having more work to complete is covered by Kevin. He could have written about the cost of training the workers to check for quality which would have been a further problem for the business. As for the benefits, it is true that the business may well sell more computers if quality was improved, though this point should have been developed further to include a possible rise in profits and bonus payments for workers if production and sales reached a particular level. Another point which could have been made is the *necessity* to improve quality to keep up with competitors, especially in a business such as computers where there are many suppliers. Kevin's answer is a good illustration of student's work which has said nothing wrong, but failed to gain even half marks.

Marks awarded – 2 out of 6

People and Organisations

SECTION 6

SOME BASICS

People can make organisations successful – or otherwise. Organisations must recruit and select workers. The process involves identifying the needs of the business, advertising the post and then gathering information about the applicants to decide who to employ. Many organisations provide extensive training for their workers in order to develop their skills and to raise productivity. They also use motivation techniques to make sure workers work to their best. These motivational techniques may involve pay but there are other ways that do not involve any payment. Finally, there are laws that organisations must obey when they employ workers. Many of these are designed to protect workers from unscrupulous employers.

Revision Material

KNOWLEDGE HIERARCHY: LIST OF THINGS TO KNOW ABOUT THE EXTERNAL ENVIRONMENT OF BUSINESS

This information is intended to provide a quick reminder. Your notes, and the information in the textbook you have used, should provide more detailed information and examples.

Topic	Key Features	Detail	Further Information
Recruitment and Selection	• Needs Analysis	• Job Description • Person Specification	• Tasks, duties • Qualifications, qualities, skills
	• Advertising the job	• Media	• Internal or external • Local/national newspapers/radio • Specialist magazines • Internet • Job centres • Word of mouth

Topic	Key Features	Detail	Further information
Recruitment and Selection *cont*.	• Selecting the worker	• Factors influencing which media used	• Cost of media • Wealth of firm • Type of worker • Location of job • Number of workers needed
		• Sources of information	• CV • Letter of application • Application form • Interview • Reference • Test • Presentations
Pay and Motivation	• Pay methods	• Hourly rate, overtime • Salary • Profit sharing • Piece rate • Commission • Bonuses • Fringe benefits	• Pay per item made • Percentage of sales • Reaching a target • Discounts on goods, etc.
	• Non-pay methods	• Job rotation • Job enlargement • Job enrichment • Team working • Award schemes • Promotion • Leadership types	• Varying the work • Adding to the job • Giving responsibility • E.g. worker of the month • Autocratic • Laissez-faire • Democratic
Training	• Needs	• New skills	• Management • Personal • Technical
	• Types of training	• Product knowledge • Group working • Flexibility • Re-training • On-the-job • Off-the-job	• Lectures • Simulations • Demonstrations • Team-building
Employment Laws and Trade Unions	• Main laws	• Equal pay • Race Discrimination	

Topic	Key Features	Detail	Further information
Employment Laws and Trade Unions *cont.*	• Main laws *cont.*	• Sex Discrimination • Health and Safety • Minimum Wage • Employment Rights	• Contract of employment
	• Benefits of unions	• Pay • Hours • Working conditions • Holidays • Unfair dismissal • Redundancy	
	• Strength of a union	• Numbers • Wealth • Type of worker • Industrial action	• Skilled vs unskilled • Strikes • Overtime ban • Work to rule

PUTTING IT IN CONTEXT

Grosvenor Lodge is a health farm in Rawcliffe. It employs 40 people. There are fitness instructors, beauticians, masseurs, nutritionists, office staff, cleaners and a handyman.

Fitness World needs to employ two additional beauticians. The General Manager, Martin Barness, who deals with *personnel* issues has drawn up a *job description* so that he is clear about the tasks that they will have to carry out and *a person specification* that describes the qualifications, skills and experience for which they are looking. To attract appropriately skilled applicants Martin included some of this information in the *advertisement*. The advertisement asked for beauticians. Fitness World really needed two female beauticians to balance the team but Martin knew it was against *equal opportunities laws* to specify female beauticians. He advertised externally in a local newspaper because the job would only interest local people, it was fairly cheap and he was confident there would be local people available. Martin interviewed a *shortlist* of five applicants.

Martin also observed each of the short-listed beauticians giving treatment so that he could assess if they had the knowledge and skills to deal with the customers.

The newly appointed beauticians were given a one-day *induction course* to introduce them to the business – its aims and objectives, the

Tests help to see if the workers have the right skills

premises and the people they would work with. Along with the other beauticians, the two new recruits also took part in a *health and safety* training session after normal hours. Martin hoped that this would prevent any accidents at work which could lead to Grosvenor Lodge being sued by one of its employees or failing a health and safety inspection because staff were not following proper procedures.

All the beauticians are *paid by the hour*. The pay is well above the *minimum national wage*. They can earn additional pay at one and half times the normal hourly rate by working *overtime* or at the weekends. To motivate the workers to provide a quality service that will maintain existing clients and attract new customers, Grosvenor Lodge also runs a *profit-sharing scheme*. Twenty-five per cent of the annual profits are shared out amongst all the employees. There is also an *Employee of the Month* Award. The worker who gains the most of these in a year receives a *bonus*. All the workers are in *teams* – the beauticians make up one team. They meet once a month to discuss any matters that concern them. Sometimes they discuss pay and conditions of work. In the three years since Grosvenor Lodge was started, the management has always responded positively to ideas and problems brought to them by the team representatives. The workers do not feel that they need to join a *trade union* to give them more influence.

 # ACTIVITIES

ACTIVITY ONE
Draw a flow chart to show the sequence of events that are likely to take place in the process of recruitment and selection of a new employee.

ACTIVITY TWO
Match up the worker with an appropriate payment method of motivation.

Worker	Payment Method of Motivation
a) Professional footballer	i) Piece rate
b) Shop assistant	ii) Profit related pay
c) General Manager of a factory	iii) Basic pay plus bonuses
d) Potter making individual pieces	iv) Commission

ACTIVITY THREE
Draw a 'consequence diagram' to show how health and safety laws affect organisations. It should show what might happen in the event of an accident leading to a claim for compensation from an employee.

ACTIVITY FOUR
Draw an image chain that represents the different types of training that a worker may receive:

Worker appointed as new recruit ⟶ worker receives technical training to develop new skills worker job shadows a manager ⟶ worker undertakes simulation training to learn how to deal with problem workers ⟶ worker studies at night school to gain extra qualifications.

Use pictures and captions to indicate the type of training, e.g. on or off the job, induction, the purpose of the training and so on.

ACTIVITIES *cont.*

ACTIVITY FIVE

Write a story of an imaginary or real dispute between workers represented by a trade union and their managers. Discuss what the dispute is about; what actions the union could use; what actions the employers could use; the role of ACAS or an Employment Tribunal in the dispute.

(NB You can research disputes for ideas – try the newspaper websites.)

QUESTION TYPES TO EXPECT

Knowledge questions that ask you to give the meaning and examples of terms such as:

- *Job descriptions and person specifications*
- *Internal and external recruitment.*
- *CVs, application forms, letters of application, interviews, tests.*
- *On and off the job training.*
- *Methods of pay – hourly rates, piece rates, commission etc.*
- *Non-pay methods of motivation – job rotation, job enrichment, team working etc.*
- *Laws affecting the employment of workers such as equal pay, race discrimination etc.*

Calculation questions will be mainly connected with pay. For example:

- *how much a worker earns calculated from hours worked, overtime rates and so on;*
- *commission payments, bonus payments;*
- *gross and net pay including calculations of deductions.*

Questions that ask you to make recommendations or judgements. Examples include:

- *What information should be included in a job advertisement?*
- *What media could be used for job advertisements, depending on the type of job, location of work, how much money the firm can afford, etc?*
- *What methods of selection are appropriate for particular types of workers – CVs or application forms, interviews or presentations, etc?*
- *Consider the suitability of different pay and non-pay methods of motivating different kinds of workers – piece rates or commission, profit sharing or bonuses.*
- *What training is appropriate to different kinds of workers or workers in different circumstances?*
- *How does an employer judge when different labour laws apply – equal pay or race discrimination? Evaluate the consequences of an event or situation.*
- *What are the benefits of trade union membership, single union agreements.*

PEOPLE IN BUSINESS: SAMPLE QUESTIONS

Question One (Higher Tier)

Burnside Engineering plc is based in Preston. It makes components for car engines. The firm needs to recruit two workers. The first is a clerical assistant. The assistant will type letters and keep records of invoices sent and paid using a computer. The second worker is a Marketing Manager who will be responsible for the marketing of the product within the European Union.

Recommend the methods of recruitment and selection that should be used in each of these appointments. Give reasons for your recommendations. **(12)**

Student Answer

The firm needs to draw up a job description and a person specification. The former will give the title of the post, any grade it is rated at, who the worker will be responsible to and the job tasks will all be stated here. The person specification looks at the type of person required and will state whether qualifications, experience, skills and any special requirements such as a valid driving licence are necessary or desirable. In this example, it is very likely that the person specifications will differ greatly as the Marketing Manager will require more qualifications and skills than a clerical assistant.

Now the firm will be ready to advertise the post. They must design each job advert carefully and they may include a selection of the following facts: a description of the job, the qualifications needed, skills needed, experience needed, salary details, hours of work, a contact number and/or future prospects at the firm so that they attract appropriate applicants. The firm must now decide whether to advertise the post internally or externally. An internally advertised post means that someone within the company will step up to the job. I would recommend this for the clerical assistant as it is a relatively small job and it is likely that someone within the company would fill this position. The advantage of employing internally is that the person will already be known to the company and so will not need a long time to adjust to their surroundings. The job could be advertised on a staff notice board or e-mailed internally to those believed to be suitable. However, for the Marketing Manager post I would recommend advertising externally due to a number of reasons. For such an important role it is likely that a person with new ideas will need to be brought in, perhaps with experience of running such an important sector.

*Due to the importance of the skills required, I would recommend advertising in a national newspaper such as **The Times** or **Telegraph** where a suitable audience would read it. A specialist magazine or radio would also be suitable. However the cost of advertising in the first mentioned can be expensive so the latter two may be more suitable, even though they reach a lesser target audience.*

When all the applicants have applied for the post, the company will then wish to draw up a shortlist of the most suitable applicants. It may first look at a letter of application which will clearly highlight the communication skills of the applicant. An application form can be used; this will help the firm to make comparisons between applicants as they will all display the same information. Finally a CV, which the applicant supplies, will also be of benefit as it is their life story displayed at a glance. I would recommend using all of these sources as they will provide a clear view of the ability and qualities of the candidates.

When the suitable candidates have been filtered out, the short list of candidates can be tested for their computer skills (for the clerical assistant) and an interview could take place which will show how well the candidate presents himself or herself. The applicant for the Marketing Manager may also be asked to give a presentation to show how well their skills are developed in this area and the ideas they have to take the firm forward.

From here the most suitable applicant for each job can be selected.

Adam

What the Examiner Says

This is as good an answer as one could expect at GCSE level under examination conditions. It is logically organised starting with the identification of needs and finishing with the selection process. There is also a lot evaluation – Adam justifies his recommendations throughout. Seems churlish to criticise, but there is more here than was needed to get the maximum marks. However, it is better to write too much than not enough.

Marks awarded – 12 out of 12

Question Two (Common Question)

Jim Smith works for Prenton's Electricals Ltd. He solders electrical circuits on to circuit boards. His pay slip for a week is shown below:

Pay Slip	**Prenton's Electricals Ltd**	Employee Number 007
Week Ending: 21 May 200_		Jim Smith

INCOME		DEDUCTIONS	
Basic Pay		Income Tax	£50
Piece Rate		National Insurance	£20
Gross Pay		Total Deductions	
Net Pay			

a) Jim Smith's basic pay is calculated at a rate of £12 for each hour he works. He worked 40 hours in the week.

He receives a piece rate of 50p for each circuit board he produces. In the week ending 21 May, he made 200 circuit boards.

Using this information and the information about deductions calculate the following:
- The basic pay
- Piece rate
- Gross pay
- Total deductions
- Net pay **(5)**

b) Explain why firms, like Prenton's Electricals Ltd, pay some workers a piece rate. **(4)**

c) Recommend **one** method involving pay that Prenton's Electricals Ltd could use for motivating the sales people that it employs. Give reasons for your recommendations. **(4)**

d) Recommend **one** method that does not involve pay that Prenton's could use to motivate the twelve office workers that it employs. Give reasons for your recommendations. **(4)**

Student Answer

a)
Basic Pay	£480
Piece Rate	£100
Gross Pay	£580
Total Deductions	£70
Net Pay	£510

b) Firms like Prenton's Electricals Ltd pay some workers a piece rate because it will motivate workers to make more because they will earn more for themselves and the business. They don't pay all the workers piece rate because they could not pay people in an office because they are not making anything to get a profit off.

c) Giving the sales people commission for every sale they make will motivate them to sell more products.

d) They could arrange staff days out, nights out and even little mini-breaks. This would motivate the office worker.

Hayley

What the Examiner Says

a) Hayley gained full marks here for the correct calculations.

Marks awarded – 5 out of 5

b) The answer is strong on the purpose of piece rates – it motivates workers to work hard and this will benefit the firm. However, Hayley does not clearly express how piece rates work. I guess she knows because of what she says about office workers, but to gain the marks Hayley needed to explain that they are a payment for each item made.

Marks awarded – 2 out of 4

c) Hayley correctly identifies that commission will motivate sales people. Again she does not fully explain what it is and how it encourages sales people. The key phrase is 'percentage of sales revenue'.

Marks awarded – 2 out of 4

d) The suggestion about nights out might work but there is no attempt to explain why this would motivate the office workers. Hayley could have developed the answer by referring to Maslow's hierarchy of needs, explaining how workers may respond positively as a result of their social needs being met. Of course there were other possible answers – worker of the month award schemes, job rotation or enlargement or enrichment. The key to a good score is to apply them to the context and explain how they would work.

Marks awarded – 1 out of 4

Question Three (Common Question)

Johnson's Chemicals Ltd specialises in the disposal of dangerous chemicals.

a) Explain **two** ways in which Johnson's Chemicals Ltd will be
   affected by employment laws. **(8)**
b) Johnson's Chemicals Ltd has a new worker who will handle the
   chemicals during the disposal process. Recommend whether the
   firm should use on-the-job or off-the-job training to train the worker. **(6)**

Student Answer

a) *Sex discrimination – This is when males or females are treated differently
because of their sex. This is a law to prevent this happening, e.g. when
advertising a job.*

*Health and Safety – This law makes it the responsibility of the employer to protect
workers from dangers in the work place.*

b) *I think the workers should do off-the-job training because it is too dangerous to train on
the job because of the dangerous chemicals that would be around. If you did not know
what you were doing it could be very dangerous.*

Rashid

What the Examiner Says

a) OCR does not require candidates to know the names of laws or Acts
of Parliament. Rashid shows that he knows what the laws are about
– sex discrimination and health and safety – and would be given
credit for this. For another mark connected with sex discrimination,
he could have explained what might happen if the business broke
the law or he could have discussed exceptional cases when males
and females can be treated differently. I would have given two
marks for the answer about health and safety, the second mark
being for clearly identifying that it is the responsibility of the
employer. For further marks, I would like to have seen Rashid
discuss health and safety inspections and/or how an employee can
sue the business in the event of an accident that is caused by the
firm's negligence which could lead to a compensation payment.

Marks awarded – 5 out of 8

b) Again Rashid makes valid points but does not explain them fully.
He could have developed an explanation of how off-the-job
training would prepare someone in a safe environment, perhaps
through simulations dealing with safe materials, before allowing
them to handle dangerous materials in a real work situation. He
could also have explained how an untrained person in a
dangerous situation might do more harm than good. Finally,
Rashid could have discussed the likelihood that health and safety
regulations would require off-the-job training before the workers
were allowed to handle chemicals in the workplace.

Marks awarded – 2 out of 6

Question Four (a) Common Question b) Higher Tier)

Salim Malik works at Birkenhead Ship Builders. He is a member of the trade union.

a) With what problems might the trade union help workers like Salim? **(4)**
b) Explain why the trade union may be better at dealing with Salim's problems than he would be on his own. **(6)**

Student Answer

a) *The trade union may help Salim if he is unfairly dismissed. It may help workers who are unhappy with pay, hours or working conditions in their job. They would also appeal if that member were made redundant. They would make sure workers had a safe environment and they would get the holiday time they needed. Some of the Acts of Parliament that could be abused are sex and race discrimination.*

b) Because it is not just one person but a body of members. The employers would be under more pressure to fulfil their demands. They offer expert advice and support because they employ specialists such as solicitors who will know what to do. They can fund expensive court cases, they employ trained negotiators who will know how to deal with the employer in question.

Josephine

What the Examiner Says

These are two very well developed answers.

a) Josephine names eight issues with which a trade union might deal for a member.

Marks awarded – 4 out of 4

b) Josephine discusses several ways in which the union is likely to have more influence than a single individual. It would also have been possible to score well by developing the 'strength through numbers' line of argument – the possibility of disruption through industrial action such as strikes, etc. and the effect of these on the competitiveness and profitability of the firm.

Marks awarded – 6 out of 6

The Changing Business Environment

SECTION 7

SOME BASICS

An increasing number of businesses sell to, or buy from, other countries. This growth of international trade has meant that the value of a currency, such as the £, becomes more important in decision-making. Profit can be seriously affected if a wrong decision is made and the exchange rate of a currency changes.

The Single Market created opportunity for increased trade with Europe

There has also been a great debate in business circles regarding the merits of being a member of the European Union, and whether to join the Single European Currency – The Euro. There are arguments on both sides; you will need to keep up-to-date with developments. What **is** certain is that international trade, in whatever form, will increase and that businesses must realise that competition can come from anywhere in the world. In some instances international trade must take place if a country requires certain products, e.g. Britain needs to import rice and bananas.

An enlarged European market will cause problems for inefficient businesses

The factors affecting business location have also changed in recent years. Incentives from both the UK government and the EU are persuading some businesses to locate in certain areas of high unemployment, though the 'older' factors of location such as transport and market are still important.

The growing number of larger businesses caused by mergers and takeovers has meant that the government takes a keen interest in making sure that the new monopolies do not act against the interests of the consumer. Mergers need not mean a monopoly being created which operates against the public interest. It may simply mean a larger business being created.

Revision Material

This information is intended to provide a quick reminder. Your notes, and the information in the textbook you have used, should provide more detailed information and examples.

The European Union and International Trade

Topic	Key Features	Detail	Further Information
Why International Trade Takes Place	• Saves costs	• Production in lowest cost countries	• Production spread worldwide
	• Geographic reasons	• Certain products need particular climate	• E.g. Fruit such as bananas
		• Raw materials only in certain places	• E.g. Diamonds
	• Consumer choice	• Consumers like to have wider choice	• Consumers now used to goods from all over the world
	• Political reasons	• May be to support another country or area	• E.g. The Commonwealth countries
Benefits of International Trade to Business	• Larger market	• More countries mean more consumers	• Spreads risk
	• More profit	• Greater sales give opportunity to increase profit	• Increased opportunity with more sales
	• Economies of scale	• Increased production will lower unit costs	• Opportunity to sell at lower prices
Problems of international Trade to Business	• Loss of jobs	• Foreign goods imported mean fewer homemade products made	• E.g. Clothing industry
	• Effect on infant industries	• New industry cannot grow	• Country may be unable to grow economically
	• More competition	• More overseas business selling in UK	• Inefficient businesses will fail
Practical Difficulties for Business in International Trade	• Language	• Printing instructions • Negotiating prices	• Costs of accurate translation • Need to hire language consultant

Topic	Key Features	Detail	Further Information
Practical Difficulties for Business in International Trade *cont*.	• Currency • Transport	• Costs of changing currency • Long distances involved add to costs	• Exchange rates change. Costs difficult to anticipate • May need specialist lorries, etc.
Protectionism	• Tariffs • Quotas • Technical	• Tax on imports • Restriction on number of imports • Laws on how goods are made	• Increases price of imports • Makes home products seem cheaper • Often a % of home market • E.g. On pollution levels from vehicles
Problems of Protectionism	• Retaliation • Price rises • Legal problems • May support inefficiency	• Other countries restrict your exports • Foreign goods cost more with tariffs • Actions taken may be illegal • Older inefficient industries survive with protection	• All countries suffer with lack of trade • Inflation increase in home country • E.g. French ban on British beef • Keeps costs high in home country
Exchange Rates	• Stable exchange rate • Rising value of £ • Falling value of £	• Exchange rates remain the same • Importers benefit • Exporters have problems • Importers have problems • Exporters benefit	• E.g. £1= €1.5 stays the same • E.g. £1= €1.5 changes to £1= €1.6 • E.g. £1= €1.5 changes to £1= €1.4
European Union (EU) Benefits of EU Membership for Business	• 15 members at present (2003) • Started in 1957 • Aim to cooperate more closely • Enlarged market	• Issues many directives which affect business • E.g. European Central Bank • More opportunity for sales and cost savings • 10 more countries to join in 2004	• E.g. Cooling off period with doorstop sales • Controls economic policy of Euro zone • Mainly from Eastern Europe

Topic	Key Features	Detail	Further Information
Benefits of EU Membership for Business *cont*.	• Single market	• Started 1 September 1993	• Easier trade within EU
	• Common standards of products	• Saves making different goods for different countries	• E.g. Electrical standards for home appliances
	• Grants and subsidies	• Helps businesses in poorer areas	• E.g. Restructuring after coal and steel closures
Problems of EU Membership for Business	• Enlarged market	• More competition may mean job losses	
	• Social Charter	• Increase costs for some business	• E.g. Minimum wage
	• Environmental standards	• More costs to meet pollution controls, etc.	• Water industry has been affected
Single European Currency	• 12 of 15 members of EU use the Euro (2003) • Use started in January 2002	• UK yet to decide	• Vote some time in the future
Advantages of Joining Single Currency	• Cost savings	• No costs of changing currency within Euro zone	• Less costs = more profit opportunity
	• Stable exchange rate	• Enables businesses to plan ahead with more certainty	
Problems of Joining Single Currency	• Adds to costs	• Cost of changing tills, etc.	
	• Loss of the £	• Britain will lose the £ as a currency	• Seen by some as a loss of control over economy
	• Difficult to reverse	• Once decision is made, very difficult to change	• Must be certain of joining

The Location of Business

Topic	Key Features	Detail	Further Information
Why Important to Business	• May be the difference between success and failure	• Once started, difficult and expensive to move again	• Choice must be carefully made
Raw Materials	• Reduce cost of expensive transport of heavy goods	• Steel works near iron ore supplies • Oil refineries on the coast	• E.g. Sheffield and South Wales steelworks • E.g. Milford Haven oil refineries
Transport	• The need to have quick deliveries in and out. Cuts costs	• Includes road, rail, air, and coastal locations • Motorway locations near junctions for easy access	• Important in delivery business • Lorries need main road location for delivery
Labour	• Important for labour intensive business	• Can mean looking worldwide for cheapest location	• E.g. Trainers made in Far East • Call centres now located worldwide
Costs	• Cost of land important	• E.g. Supermarkets need large areas of flat land, cost is vital	• Land cheaper in northern England • Edge of cities cheaper than centre
Government Aid	• Incentives for location in certain areas	• High unemployment areas targeted	• Some areas often unattractive without incentives
Near to Market	• Cuts cost of transport to customers	• Affects many businesses • Some goods need to be fresh	• E.g. Most shops, bakeries
Traditions	• Once established, difficult to move	• Location name may help product • Skills in area for future workers	• Sheffield steel an example
Enterprise Zones	• Small areas giving advantages to business	• Simplfied planning • Tax allowances • No Business Rates for 10 years • Help with training • Infrastructure improvements	• Can greatly reduce business costs • May lead to poor location being chosen if costs the only consideration
Assisted Areas	• Larger areas receiving aid	• Rural areas benefit • Former coal and steel areas targeted	• Receive less assistance than Enterprise Zones

Topic	Key Features	Detail	Further Information
Regional Development Agencies	• Co-ordinate investment	• Local skills improved • Advice on aid applications • Improvements to local environment • Help economic regeneration	• Workers may need training in new skills • Great help to smaller business with advice

Types of Market

Topic	Key Features	Detail	Further Information
Competition	• Many buyers and sellers of products and services	• Businesses usually small • No one business influences others • Great choice for consumer	• Easy to set up in business • Businesses compete on price and service • E.g. Small 'corner' shops
Oligopoly	• A few firms control most sales	• Usually much larger businesses • Often 'agree' on prices • Actions of one followed by others	• E.g. Petrol companies • Compete on promotions and location
Monopoly	• One producer controls at least 25% of sales	• Business may produce one product • Little real competition • Consumer has little choice • However, can benefit consumer	• Prices may be higher with less choice • Prices could be lower with economies of scale
Government and Competition	• The Law	• European Union directives • Price fixing illegal • Forcing prices up by selling less is illegal	
	• Office of Fair Trading	• Tries to encourage competition	
	• Watchdogs	• Control the former Public Utilities e.g. Electricity	• Price and service levels monitored
	• Competition Commission	• Checks if mergers are in the public interest	• Checks on actions of possible monopolies

PUTTING IT IN CONTEXT

Doultwedge plc is a pottery business, specialising in high quality pottery and china. For many years it has *exported* products throughout the world, realising that a *larger market* will not only *spread the risks* of the business, but also give the opportunity of *economies of large scale production*. Whilst cutting *unit costs* for the business, there was the possibility of *increasing profit*.

In recent years, *international trade* has meant that *cheaper imports* have taken some of the trade from Doultwedge plc. There have been some *job losses* at their main factory in Oldcastle as a result of this *competition*. Because Doultwedge plc is not an inefficient business, they feel they have a good future. The management see no need for *tariffs* or *quotas to restrict the imports* as this would possibly mean *retaliation* from the countries to which Doultwedge plc exported.

The business is hoping to start exporting to new countries, but understands that there will be *extra costs* in doing this, notably *new language brochures* and the *extra costs of transport*. The possible expansion of the *European Union* will certainly be a new *target market* for the company.

UK membership of the *EU* influenced the introduction of the *minimum wage* into the country. This had less effect on Doultwedge plc than other local businesses. They already paid their workers above the *minimum level* and so had no concern about *rising costs* which were affecting some of their competitors.

Recent rises in the *value of the £* against other currencies have meant *exporting* is proving more difficult for the business. These *exchange rate changes* have meant that *exports have become dearer* in countries to which Doultwedge plc sells. The company would like to see Britain joining the *Single European Currency* (Euro) as this would help *stabilise exchange rates* and *make future planning clearer*.

The main factory site was *located* in Oldcastle nearly 200 years ago because the necessary *raw material* (clay) was found nearby. Over the years *local labour* developed the necessary high levels of skills required for the business. The local clay has now all but run out, but the *location* has not been moved as the local pottery *tradition* has meant that the 'Made in Oldcastle' helps sell the pottery and it would be *costly to move* and retrain a new workforce elsewhere.

Possible future expansion of the business to include a craft shop and tour centre for schools may well attract *Government support*, as Oldcastle is in an *Assisted Area* due to the *high levels of employment* in the local area.

Other possibilities in the future would be the *merger* of Doultwedge plc and Girldro plc, though this would create a *monopoly*, as the enlarged business would control more than *25% of the pottery market*. Such a move would mean that there would be an investigation by the *Competition Commission* in order to see if the merger was in the *interests of the consumer*.

 # ACTIVITIES

ACTIVITY ONE

For each of the following businesses, explain the factors that would be considered in choosing a suitable location for the business:

- A factory making trainers.
- A mail order delivery centre.
- A hypermarket.
- A fish and chip shop.
- A research laboratory concentrating on the development of new drugs.
- A factory which freezes fresh vegetables.

ACTIVITY TWO

When the exchange rate of the £ changes, there is an effect on both importers and exporters. Complete the following flow consequence diagram to explain the results of the changes. The first has been started for you.

Draw similar consequence diagrams for b) and c):

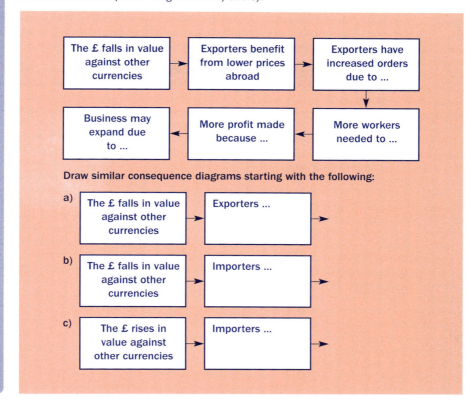

ACTIVITY THREE

Many industries in Britain have changed due to international trade and competition.

a) Look around your house and find at least 10 products, such as clothing, electrical goods, furniture, etc. Look where each of the products was made

b) Draw a bar graph to show your results. Use three categories for your graph, made in the UK, made in Europe, made in the rest of the world. Comment on the findings shown in the graph.

c) Choose any three products that are made *outside* the UK. Explain why these are imported and then bought in the UK, rather than being home produced.

Many goods we now buy are imported

ACTIVITY FOUR

Complete the following chart to explain the problems and benefits of membership of the European Union. Make your chart large enough for detailed explanations. Some features may be in both benefits and problem columns; others will only be in one.

Feature	Benefit because...	Problem because...
Enlarged market		
Single market		
Social Charter		
Environmental standards		
Common standards for products		
Grants and subsidies		

ACTIVITY FIVE

In October 2002 Granada Television and Carlton Television announced they would like to merge. Before this could happen, the Competition Commission would have to agree.

ACTIVITIES *cont.*

a) What does the Competition Commission do?

b) Why should the Competition Commission be involved in this merger of two television companies?

c) With the help of your teacher, try and find other mergers that are taking place now. Explain why or why not the Competition Commission is involved in the merger.

 QUESTION TYPES TO EXPECT

Questions that ask you to give the meaning and examples of terms such as:

- *Tariffs*
- *Quotas*
- *Exchange rates*
- *Social Charter*
- *European Union*
- *Single European Currency*
- *Importers and Exporters*
- *Monopoly*
- *Oligopoly*
- *Competition*
- *Assisted Areas*
- *Enterprise Zones*
- *Competition Commission*
- *'Watchdogs'*
- *Office of Fair Trading*

There are many practical problems in international trade

More difficult questions that you may be asked:

- *Identify and explain the benefits and problems caused by international trade.*
- *Explain the effects of cheaper imported goods on particular industries in the UK.*
- *Evaluate the merits of protectionism in international trade.*
- *Evaluate the benefits and problems caused by the UK's membership of the European Union.*
- *Calculate the effects of a change in the value of the £ to both importers and exporters.*
- *Interpret and evaluate numerical data relating to exchange rate changes.*

- *Identify and explain the problems and benefits of joining the Single European Currency.*
- *Analyse the reasons why businesses locate in particular areas.*
- *Explain the role of government in business location decisions.*
- *Identify and explain the differences between different types of market.*
- *Explain how and why the UK government takes an interest in large business mergers and takeovers.*
- *Explain the possible advantages and disadvantages of competitive markets to the consumer.*
- *Explain the possible advantages and disadvantages of monopolies to the consumer.*

Some examples of these types of questions and student answers are given in the following section. Look carefully at what the question is asking you to do; how the student has answered the question; what the examiner thinks of the answer.

THE CHANGING BUSINESS ENVIRONMENT: SPECIMEN QUESTIONS

Question one (a)
Common Question
b) Higher Tier

Printit Ltd export calendars and diaries to different countries throughout the world.

a) Explain **two** possible benefits to Printit Ltd of exporting to different countries. **(4)**

b) Explain how the following might affect Printit Ltd:
   i) Other countries putting tariffs on imports.
   ii) Other countries putting quotas on imports. **(6)**

Student Answer

a)   If Printit Ltd do export to different countries they are taking a market share in different markets besides their own, this can give them support in harder times if their own market economy is not doing so well. Also they can hire people to work in different countries, if they can find the suitable skilled workers – they would need to have language qualifications, the job would be made more desirable as it would be in a different country.

b) If a country that Printit exports to puts a tariff on their imports this would cause the Printit product to be more expensive than the native products and hence causing Printit's profit from that country to fall as people would be buying the cheaper native goods.

If a country did put a quota on imports it would limit the amount Printit could sell in that country and due to that Printit's profits would be in turn limited.

Mark

What the Examiner Says

a) Mark has correctly identified one benefit, that of spreading risk. If the economy of one country is in decline, then exports sales in other countries would indeed help the business. In the second example there seems to be some confusion as the answer seems to suggest workers producing the goods in different countries. This has no real connection with the question which asks for the benefits of exporting to different countries.

A further example which outlined the benefits from increased production and so reduction of costs (economies of scale) would have gained full marks.

Marks awarded – 2 out of 4

b) Mark has correctly identified the fact that an introduction of tariffs will increase the price of imports, which will mean (possibly) lower profits as consumers will switch to the lower priced 'native' products. In fact consumers may well buy the imports at a higher price if home products are inferior. This however is not certain.

Quotas will mean a lowering of the amount of goods Printit Ltd will be able to export. There is once again the potential for lower profits, as identified by Mark, though this is not developed. Printit Ltd might, in fact, be able to put up the price of their products if there is sufficient demand.

Marks awarded – 5 out of 6

Question two (Higher Tier)

JMY Ltd makes light fittings which are exported to the European Union.

a) Explain the possible problems of European Union membership to a business such as JMY Ltd. The market for light fittings is very competitive. **(6)**

b) The value of the Euro to the £ has increased from £1 = €1.5, to £1 = €1.7. Explain how this change in value of the Euro might affect JMY Ltd. **(6)**

Student Answer

a) *There is a lot of competition for light fittings, which means that JMY Ltd must be very careful about increasing their prices, otherwise this will mean that they lose customers. As Britain is in the EU, other businesses abroad can export their goods easily to Britain without any restrictions. This will mean that JMY has even more competition and may lose business. The EU introduce laws and directives which affect businesses. This might affect the way they work and increase costs, such as the minimum wage, and the working time directive, which puts a limit on the hours an employee should work.*

b) *If the price of the pound has increased abroad then it would cause the price of all JMY's products that are exported to different countries who have the Euro to increase. This would cause the profits in that country, which is importing the products to drop as JMY's product, will be more expensive than its competitors. For instance if the product was priced at €3 a fall in the value of the Euro would increase the price of the same product to €3.4.*

Katy

What the Examiner Says

a) The answer given by Katy centres upon two ideas; competition and laws. Both these ideas are well developed with examples given as to how they impact upon the business. The examples of the minimum wage and working time directive are well chosen.

Marks awarded – 6 out of 6

b) Katy has correctly identified that this change in value of the £ against the Euro will affect *all* the countries which are in the Euro zone. It is also correct to say that the price of the product will increase in the Euro zone, even giving a correct mathematical example. The fall in profits of the country importing the goods is a little confusing and not fully linked to an effect on Printit Ltd.

Katy could have explored the connection between a rise in the cost of the light fittings abroad and a fall in demand which in turn would have meant fewer orders. This may then have led to some workers being laid off, or new markets having to be found outside the Euro zone which are not affected by currency changes etc.

Marks awarded – 3 out of 6

Question Three (Common Question)

Oscar Ltd supply parts for computers. They promise next day delivery on parts which are ordered before 5pm. The management at Oscar Ltd are looking for a new location for the parts warehouse. Explain how the following might affect the decision on where to locate the new warehouse.

a) Government aid
b) Transport links to the warehouse **(6)**

Student Answer

a) *Oscar Ltd locate their warehouse in a redevelopment area then it is possible to receive government aid, this is offered to entice businesses to set up their business here and make jobs for the local residents. This will influence Oscar Ltd because they will have to take into account the opportunity of receiving aid for just setting up their warehouse in a certain area.*

b) *As Oscar Ltd promise next day delivery, they must make sure they are next to transport links that can make this possible. The best place to locate would be next to a busy motorway junction, where more than two motorways meet. This will mean that lorries can get in and out to deliver the parts quickly and Oscar Ltd can keep their promise. If this was next to a large city it would be even better as this is where the customers will be for the computer parts. This would help cut time for delivery (and costs) even more.*

Suzanne

What the Examiner Says

a) Suzanne has recognised that governments 'entice' businesses to particular areas by giving aid, which will be to the benefit of the business itself and local residents. This will indeed be considered by the business, though the answer could have been more precise with an example such as relief from Business Rates and how this will reduce the costs of the business.

b) This is a much better answer with a clear link being made to the benefits of good transport links (motorway junction, just outside large cities) for a business which must deliver (and collect for delivery) items the next day. The link between time and costs is well made.

Marks awarded – 5 (2 + 3) out of 6

Question Four (Higher Tier)

Evaluate the considerations a foreign car manufacturer such as Nissan and Toyota might make in deciding on a location for a new car production centre.

(8)

Student Answer

If either Nissan or Toyota did decide to place a new car plant in the UK then there would be obvious benefits such as government aid offered to them to attract them to certain parts of the country where there is high unemployment. As they would need large amounts of both skilled and unskilled workers then the government would offer them a great deal of aid to set up their plant in a certain area so that the government can say they have reduced unemployment in that area due to the new car plant offering large amounts of employment.

Also they, too, would have to think about transporting their cars across the country to their many showrooms so that the cars can be sold to the public. This would influence them because they wouldn't want to set up their car plant in an area that didn't have good transportation links to the rest of the country.

Both these factors contribute to the decision-making of where to set up a car plant. It is the board of directors of both companies jobs to make a compromise between the two, if one should arise that is. For instance it would be useless setting up a car plant in the middle of nowhere just so that the company can receive government aid.

Conrad

What the Examiner Says

The command word in this question is 'evaluate'. This means that a judgement must be made as to the factors that have the *greatest* influence *in this particular case*.

Conrad has judged correctly that this particular business will be of considerable size, requiring large amounts of skilled and unskilled labour, which would itself attract government aid if located in certain areas. This particular business would also require the stated transport links to transport the finished goods to market.

Whilst this identification of the factors affecting location is good (the sheer size of the required site could have been included) the *evaluation* of the factors is rather lacking. A general statement is made that the company should not consider a place just because it receives aid, but this is not developed. Conrad should have considered importance the different factors he identified and made a judgement as to which are the more important, giving reasons for that decision.

This answer is at the lower part of Level 2 (5–8 marks). Further evaluation is necessary, with reasons, to move further into this Level.

3

PART THREE

CASE STUDY

OCR offers candidates the choice of doing coursework or sitting an examination called the Case Study Paper.

The pre-seen Case Study material will be sent to the centre about six months before the examination. Students and teachers need to work together on these materials. The most important job is to try to spot the types of questions that are likely to come up. A good way to do this is to think like an examiner. When the examiner writes the Case Study material, he or she will be thinking of possible questions that they might ask. Having written the case study, the examiner will then draft out possible questions. In the Case Study below, the notes that the examiner made as he worked on the data are shown in italics on a coloured background.

You should make notes like the examiners and then try to write your own questions. Twenty possible questions are given below the Case Study material as an illustration. Remember that because the coursework does not test knowledge, the Case Study will not test this skill. This means that there will be no questions asking for the meanings of terms. The questions in the case study will focus on application, analysis and evaluation. You should bear in mind that the examiner will be trying to set questions on all the different sections of the Business Studies GCSE specification. You might find it useful to refer back to the 'Types of Questions' in each section in Part 2 of the book to help you to think of likely questions.

What questions will be asked?

 ## CASE STUDY MATERIAL

Fitness World is a leisure complex in the town of Rawcliffe. It opened three years ago. The owners are Fitness World Ltd. The cost of the leisure complex was £6m. The finance of the complex was partly covered by a government grant of £1m.

Possibility of question re source of finance and form of ownership and why governments give grants.

It was built on a town centre brownfield site and a part of Coronation Park, an area of lawns and trees with a duck pond and children's play area. The complex contains a swimming pool and a gymnasium. There is also a large bar area in the premises. At the time that Fitness World Ltd sought planning permission for the development, there were strong feelings in the local community, both for and against giving the go-ahead.

Possibility of question re stakeholders and social costs and benefits.

The General Manager, Catherine Charlton, drew up the following diagram. It is the Organisation Chart for Fitness World.

Possibility of lots of questions re Organisation Charts – why draw them up, short questions re span of control/who is responsible to whom/number of layers, general description, problems of structure/communications, etc.

Organisation Chart – Fitness World

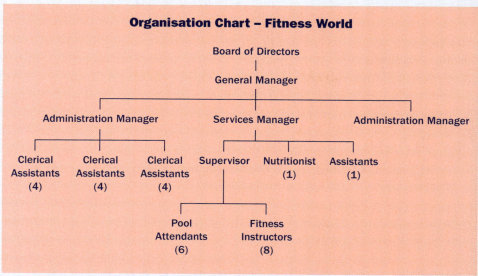

Board of Directors

General Manager

Administration Manager — Services Manager — Administration Manager

Clerical Assistants (4) Clerical Assistants (4) Clerical Assistants (4) Supervisor Nutritionist (1) Assistants (1)

Pool Attendants (6) Fitness Instructors (8)

Before the start of its first year of trading, Catherine and the Marketing Manager, Desmond Ogono, projected the following regarding revenues and costs.

Revenues *The owners had decided that the complex would be a member-only club targeted at the more wealthy sections of the local community. They believed that the local council leisure complex made provision for the middle and lower income groups in the community. They decided to charge an annual subscription fee of £500 per head which would allow unrestricted, free entry at any time.*

Costs *The following table shows a summary of projected costs and revenues:*

Number of Members	Fixed Costs	Variable Costs	Total Costs	Revenue
100	98,000	15,000	113,000	50,000
200	98,000	30,000	128,000	100,000
300	98,000	45,000	143,000	150,000
400	98,000	60,000	158,000	200,000
500	98,000	75,000	173,000	250,000

At the end of the first year, Fitness World had 320 members.

Possibility of break-even, margin of safety, types of costs, controlling costs, forecasts and problems of them and some information that might be relevant for some marketing questions, for example: Are there enough members? Is there a profit/enough profit?

The Marketing Manager decided that Fitness World needed to be marketed differently in order to raise total revenue. One decision was to employ six more fitness instructors who would offer a range of exercise classes for different market segments.

Setting up question/s on recruitment and selection.

Setting up questions on what the different segments may be, also recommendations for other marketing strategies – pricing, promotions, etc.

Another development that was put in place was to change the bar area into a bakery and café that would sell lunches and snacks.

Possibility of a question on appropriate production methods – for cakes, freshly baked bread, ready made meals, etc. – may need some more information here. Also how should the café be run/owned?

The Profit and Loss Accounts for Fitness World for its second and third year of trading are shown below:

	Year 2 £ 000s	Year 3 £ 000s
Sales Revenue	800	1 000
less Cost of Sales	80	100
GROSS PROFIT	**720**	**900**
less Expenses	640	800
NET PROFIT BEFORE TAX	**80**	**100**
Tax	32	40
NET PROFIT AFTER TAX	**48**	**60**
Retained Profit	40	50
Available for distribution to Shareholders	8	10

Extract from the Trading Profit and Loss Account for Fitness World Ltd for the periods ending 31 December

Possibility of questions re accounts – comparison/evaluation of Year 3 against Year 2, more detailed questions re specific parts of the accounts.

Twenty possible questions on the case study material

1. Suggest, giving reasons, some possible sources of finance which Fitness World Ltd might have used to finance the building of a new leisure complex in Rawcliffe.

2. Although Fitness World Ltd is a privately owned company, explain the possible reason why the government would have given it a £1m grant to build the leisure complex.

3. Explain possible advantages and drawbacks of Fitness World Ltd operating as a private limited company.

4. The local newspaper is preparing a feature about the leisure complex to coincide with the third anniversary of its opening. You have been asked to provide some information for the feature. Write an account detailing the social costs and benefits which the leisure complex may have brought to the local area.

5. Study the Organisation Chart for Fitness World and explain the possible advantages and disadvantages of the present organisational structure.

6. The management of Fitness World is considering changing the organisational structure as it is felt that the Chain of Command is too long. Evaluate whether it is better for a business such as this to have a long Chain of Command or a wide Span of Control.

7. Recommend appropriate ways in which the management of Fitness World can communicate information to its employees.

8. The Services Manager will shortly be leaving the company. A new manager will need to be recruited. Outline the steps, in the form of a flow chart, which the firm will take to fill the vacancy.

9. Draw up a list of the skills and qualities which Fitness World may be looking for in the Fitness Instructors which it is looking to recruit.

10. a) Using the revenue and cost information provided, draw up a break-even forecast for Fitness World when it started trading.
    b) What is the break-even level of output?
    c) Explain why businesses such as Fitness World carry out break-even analysis calculations.
    d) Explain why the forecast that Fitness World has made may not be totally accurate.

11. Membership has not been as high as Fitness World hoped when it started the business. Recommend a marketing strategy which the business may be able to use.

12. Fitness World has decided to introduce a new membership category aimed at those people aged over 55. Explain why the business may have decided to target this particular segment of the market and whether or not it is likely to be a good idea.

13. Fitness World charged all members an annual fee of £500 which then gave unrestricted use of the leisure centre. Recommend alternative pricing strategies that Fitness World may use to try to raise revenue.

14. Explain, giving examples, why it is important for a business to control its costs.

15. Recommend to Fitness World whether they should offer the bakery and café as a franchise or operate the business themselves.

16. The bakery produces a range of different kinds of bread each day. Recommend an appropriate method of production for making the bread. Give reasons for your answer.

17. Using the information in the Profit and Loss Account, evaluate the financial performance of the business over the last two years.

18. Study the Gross Profit and Net Profit before Tax figures for the business. Analyse if there is any difference between these figures for Years 2 and 3.

19. Explain why the business may have decided to retain most of the profit it has made.

20. Explain why the government collects tax from the profits made by companies such as Fitness World.

How many of these questions had you thought of? Read them again looking carefully at the command words in each question and at the variety of questions asked on similar topics.

4

PART FOUR

OCR BUSINESS STUDIES GCSE – SAMPLE QUESTIONS DIFFERENTIATED IN TERMS OF DIFFICULTY

This part of the book gives a selection of questions from recent past papers and the specimen paper for the specifications introduced for first examination in 2003. They are organised according to the part of the specification that they relate to. Some slight amendments have been made to the wording of some of the questions so that they work as 'stand alone' questions – in particular, detail about the context that the question applies to has been added or repeated in the stem to the question.

The External Environment of Business

SECTION 1

A*-B Questions

1998

Carlton Press Ltd is a small publishing company. It imports paper from Germany.

i)   How might a fall in the exchange rate of the Pound Sterling against the Euro from £1 = 3 Euros to £1 = 2 Euros affect the price of paper? **(2)**
ii) What could Carlton Press Ltd do if the exchange rate fell? **(2)**
iii) How may membership of the European Union help UK businesses to trade with businesses in other member countries? **(6)**
iv) What disadvantages might the UK's membership of the European Union bring to British firms? **(4)**

1999

The table below shows the levels of employment by sector, in 1968 and 1998, in the economy of the town of Bowton.

Working Population by Sector
Economy of Bowton

	1968	1998
Primary Sector	1000	500
Secondary Sector	9000	4000
Tertiary Sector	10,000	16,000

i)   Describe the main changes in the levels of employment by sector that have taken place between 1968 and 1998. **(4)**
ii) Explain why the changes in employment in the secondary sector may have occurred. **(4)**
iii) Are the changes in employment that have taken place a problem for the people of Bowton? Give reasons for your answer. **(8)**

C-D Questions

2000

a) Jason Lee works for Colliers PLC, which makes and sells chocolates, in the town of Marston. His friend, Alison Stone, works for the Education Department of Marston Borough Council.
   i) Using the evidence above, explain why Marston is a mixed economy. **(2)**
   ii) State **two** appropriate objectives for Colliers PLC and **two** appropriate objectives for the Education Department? Use the table below for your answer. **(4)**
b) Explain fully how Colliers PLC may benefit other businesses in the Marston area. **(4)**

2001

TechWorld Ltd is a chain of shops. The shops sell computer hardware and software including games. It plans to build and open new shops across the Midlands.

Explain how the new shops in the chain may benefit the following:

- The people who live in the areas where the shops are built.
- Other businesses in the areas where the shops are built. **(8)**

E-G Questions

Jason Lee works for Colliers PLC, which makes and sells chocolates, in the town of Marston. His friend, Alison Stone, works for the Education Department of Marston Borough Council.

i) Which person works in the public sector and which in the private sector of the economy? **(2)**

ii) Below is a list of possible objectives that organisations may have. Which **two** are likely to be objectives of Colliers PLC and which **two** are likely to be objectives of the Education Department? Tick the appropriate boxes below to give your answer. **(4)**

Objective	Colliers PLC	Education Department
Provide schooling for all children of school-age in Marston.		
Sell as many goods as possible.		
Make as much profit as possible.		
Prepare young people for the world of work.		

iii) State **two** ways in which Colliers PLC may be of benefit to each of the following:
- The people who live in Marston.
- Other businesses in the Marston area. **(4)**

2001

TechForce Ltd manufactured personal computers. TechWorld Ltd bought the computers from TechForce Ltd and retailed them.

i) State which firm belonged to the secondary sector of the economy and which to the tertiary sector. Give a reason for each answer. **(4)**

ii) State **four** business objectives that TechForce Ltd may have. **(4)**

2002

The business that runs Bowton Airport has made a planning application to the local council to extend the runway and build a new terminal so that it can cope with more flights in the future.

State and explain the benefits and the problems that the local council should take into consideration when deciding whether or not to approve the planning application. **(8)**

Business Structure, Organisation and Control

SECTION 2

A*-B Questions

1998

Carlton Press Ltd publishes educational books. The following is the organisation chart for Carlton Press Ltd.

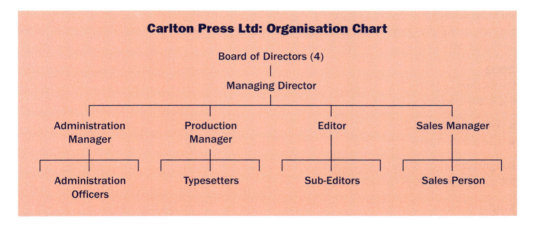

Carlton Press Ltd: Organisation Chart

Board of Directors (4)

Managing Director

Administration Manager — Production Manager — Editor — Sales Manager

Administration Officers — Typesetters — Sub-Editors — Sales Person

Describe the main features of the internal organisation of Carlton Press Ltd. **(8)**

1999

David Norris runs a market stall in Bowton, Jeans and Ts, selling jeans and T-shirts. It is a sole trader business. The business has been quite successful in recent years and he is considering expanding by opening another stall in a second market. Should David keep the business as a sole trader? Use your knowledge of the advantages and disadvantages of the different forms of business. **(9)**

2000

Some of the retailers that sell Colliers PLC's chocolates are small, independent sole traders. Colliers, which manufactures chocolates and sells some of its produce through its own chain of retail outlets, is a PLC. Are these appropriate forms of ownership for these different businesses? Give reasons for your answer. **(7)**

2001

In March 2001 the owners of TechWorld Ltd decided that the business should go into liquidation. The figures below show the value of the assets and the debts of TechWorld Ltd at this time.

TechWorld Ltd	
Assets and Debts – March 2001	
Value of Assets	£24m
Value of Debts	£32m

i)   Explain the meaning of the term 'going into liquidation.'   **(2)**
ii) As the owners of a limited company, the shareholders of TechWorld Ltd enjoy the benefits of limited liability. Using the figures above, illustrate how the shareholders will benefit.   **(4)**

2002

Dream Days Ltd is a travel firm which organises and sells special event trips and holidays such as shopping weekends in Paris and trips to major sporting events. It is planning to expand. The owners are considering changing the firm to a Public Limited Company. Explain whether or not this would be a good idea for the business. Give reasons for your answer.   **(6)**

2002

Dream Days Ltd plans to spend £5m to buy a plane to use for some of its holidays. It may finance this in the following ways:

- Take out a bank loan.
- Use retained profit.

Recommend which of the above methods Dream Days Ltd should use to finance the purchase of the plane. Give reasons for your choice.   **(6)**

C–D Questions

1998

i)   State and explain how the status of Carlton Press Ltd, as a limited company, will help it to raise the finance necessary for investments such as buying new technology.   **(4)**
ii) State and explain one disadvantage of being a private limited company.   **(4)**

2000

Explain the meaning of the following terms:

- Shareholders
- Dividends   **(4)**

2000

a) Jason Lee worked for Colliers PLC, a firm that manufactures and retails chocolate. He is leaving Colliers PLC and intends to open a shop selling chocolates and sweets. Should he open the shop as a franchise or as an independent shop? Discuss the advantages and disadvantages of each option to give reasons for your answer.   **(8)**
b) If Jason Lee opened his shop as a sole trader, explain how he might finance the purchase of the shop and its fittings.   **(4)**

2001

SoftSolutions is a partnership owned by Martin and Helen Dean.

i)   Explain why the owners of partnerships often draw up a Deed of Partnership.   **(4)**
ii) State and explain **two** advantages to Martin and Helen of setting up the business as a
     partnership.   **(4)**

2001

In March 2001 the owners of TechWorld Ltd decided that the business should go into liquidation.
The figures below show the value of the assets and the debts of TechWorld Ltd at this time.

TechWorld Ltd	
Assets and Debts – March 2001	
Value of Assets	£24m
Value of Debts	£32m

i)   Calculate the value of the debts that would remain unpaid after the assets have been sold
     after the business went into liquidation.   **(2)**
ii) As the owners of a limited company, the shareholders of TechWorld Ltd enjoy the benefits of
     limited liability. Using the figures above, illustrate how the shareholders will benefit.   **(4)**

2001

The table below shows possible methods of finance available to businesses.

Methods of Finance

Time Period	Method of Finance
Short Term	Overdraft; Trade Credit
Medium Term	Hire Purchase; Bank Loan
Long Term	Shares; Debentures

TechWorld Ltd is a chain of shops selling computers, software and computer games.

Recommend **one** method of finance that TechWorld Ltd should use for each of the situations. Give
reasons for your answers.

a)   To build more shops at a cost of £3m.
b)   To pay for more stocks of computer games to sell in the shops.
c)   To deal with a cash flow problem caused by low sales in the summer months.   **(9)**

2002

Dream Days Ltd is a travel firm which organises and sells special event trips and holidays such as
shopping weekends in Paris and trips to major sporting events. The shareholders who own Dream
Days Ltd have limited liability. Explain why this is an advantage to shareholders.   **(4)**

E-G QUESTIONS

1998

Carlton Press Ltd publishes educational books. Using the words below, complete the following
statements about the sources of finance that Carlton Press Ltd could use.

BANK LOAN   SHARES   OVERDRAFT   LEASING

An _____ is when the bank allows the business to spend more than is in its current account.

_____ is when the business rents equipment over a period of time.

A _____ is when the bank lends an amount of money to the business for a fixed period of time.

Carlton Press Ltd can sell _____ to raise extra finance.   **(4)**

1998

Carlton Press Ltd publishes educational books. The following is the organisation chart for Carlton Press Ltd.

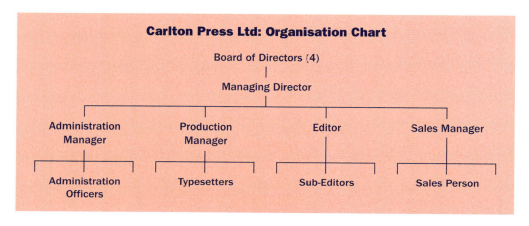

i)   Who is the line manager of the typesetters?   **(1)**
ii) What is the span of control of the Managing Director?   **(1)**
iii) Use the following words to complete the sentences below:

          FUNCTION   DELEGATED   SUBORDINATE   LAYERS

There are four _____ in the organisation.
The Production Manager is a _____ of the Managing Director.
The departments are organised by _____.
The Managing Director has _____ responsibility to the
department managers.   **(4)**

iv) What are the benefits to Carlton Press Ltd of having a specialist Sales Manager? **(2)**

2000

Use the phrases below to help to explain the meaning of the terms dividend and shareholder.

- a payment made to shareholders
- an owner of a business
- the amount paid depending on how much profit the business makes
- takes a risk by putting money into the business   **(4)**

2000

What do the letters PLC stand for? **(1)**

The following are features of PLCs and sole traders. Place them under the correct heading.

a) able to sell shares on the Stock Exchange
b) owned by one person
c) the owner has limited liability
d) can have any number of shareholders

Features of a PLC	Features of a Sole Trader

(4)

2001

SoftSolutions is a partnership. Place a tick in the boxes given below to say whether the following statements are true or false about partnerships.

Statement	True	False
A partnership has shareholders.		
A partnership usually has between 2 and 20 owners.		
Partners often draw up a deed of partnership that states how profits will be shared out.		
Partners often use their own savings to set up a business.		
The partners cannot employ people to work for them.		
At least one partner has unlimited liability for any debts the business has should it be declared bankrupt.		

(6)

Business Behaviour – Marketing

SECTION 3

A*–B Questions

1998

Carlton Press Ltd sell educational books in different market segments.

i) What is meant by the term 'market segments'? **(2)**
ii) Describe **two** market segments to which Carlton Press Ltd may sell books. **(4)**

1999

David runs a stall, Jeans and Ts, selling jeans and T-shirts. It is located in the town of Bowton. His wife, Shona, plans to open a similar stall in the nearby town of Mencaster. Market research has provided the following information about Mencaster and Bowton.

Information about Mencaster and Bowton

	Mencaster	Bowton
Population	90,000	40,000
Social Classes	A,B,C1: 10%	A, B, C1: 55%
	C2, D, E: 90%	C2, D, E: 45%
Average Annual Income per person	£14,000	£28,000
Unemployment Rate	10%	5%

Should the marketing strategy that Shona uses in Mencaster be different from that of David in Bowton? Support your answer with information from the market research data. **(12)**

2000

Colliers PLC plans to produce a chocolate bar made of white chocolate and filled with nuts and caramel. It intends to target its marketing at people who are keen on keeping fit.

Recommend a strategy for marketing the new bar. Give reasons for your recommendations. **(12)**

C–D Questions

1998

Carlton Press Ltd sell a GCSE Business Studies textbook.

a) Market research has provided the following information for Carlton Press Ltd.
   - 75% of candidates for the GCSE Business Studies examination buy a textbook.

- Carlton Press Ltd gains a 20% share of the market in an average year.
- Estimated entries for GCSE Business Studies in 1999 are 160,000.

How many Business Studies textbooks books should Carlton Press Ltd plan to sell? Show your working. **(4)**

b) One method that Carlton Press Ltd use for advertising the GCSE textbook is to send leaflets to teachers in schools. Why is this a good way to advertise this book? **(2)**

c) State **one** other method of advertising that Carlton Press Ltd could use to tell the teachers about the book. Give reasons for your choice. **(2)**

2002

Dream Days Ltd is a travel firm which organises and sells special event trips and holidays such as shopping weekends in Paris and trips to major sporting events.

Dream Days Ltd sells a one-day trip from Bowton Airport to Monaco for people who want to watch the Formula 1 motor racing grand prix. The trip will cost customers £195.

Recommend the types of media that Dream Days Ltd should use to advertise this trip. Give reasons for your recommendations. **(8)**

E–G Questions

1998

Carlton Press Ltd publish educational books. The figures in the table estimate the number of Business Studies textbooks that will be sold in the UK in the next three years.

i) Using the figures in the table above, what is likely to happen to the sales of GCSE Business Studies textbooks by Carlton Press Ltd during the period? **(2)**

ii) Explain how the following might affect the numbers of books that Carlton Press Ltd sells in Year 1.
- A competitor goes out of business.
- A cut in government spending on education. **(2)**

Estimated Sales of GCSE Business Studies Textbooks: Years 1–3

Year	Estimated Sales
1	100,000
2	125,000
3	132,000

1999

David runs a stall, Jeans and Ts, selling jeans and T-shirts. It is located in the town of Bowton. His wife, Shona, plans to open a similar stall in the nearby town of Mencaster. Market research has provided the following information about Mencaster and Bowton.

Information about Mencaster and Bowton

	Mencaster	Bowton
Population	90,000	40,000
Social Classes	Middle Class: 10%	Middle Class: 55%
	Working Class: 90%	Working Class: 45%
Average Annual Income per person	£14,000	£28,000
Unemployment Rate	10%	5%

i)   Calculate how many people are unemployed in Mencaster. Show your working. **(2)**
ii) Should Shona charge a higher or lower price than David for the jeans and T-shirts that they sell? Give reasons for your answer. **(4)**
iii) What media should Shona use to advertise her new stall? Give reasons for your answer. **(4)**
iv) How would knowledge of the following help Shona to market the stall?
   ● The prices charged by her competitors.
   ● Where her competitors are located.
   ● What products her competitors sell.
   ● How many competitors she has. **(4)**

2000

a) The following diagram shows the typical product life cycle for a good or service.

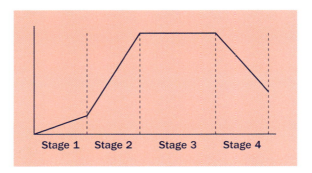

Name the four stages of the product life cycle shown.

Stage 1 _____

Stage 2 _____

Stage 3 _____

Stage 4 _____

b) Colliers PLC plans to produce a bar made of white chocolate and filled with nuts and caramel. It intends to target people who are keen on keeping fit in its marketing.
   i)   Recommend a name for the bar. Give reasons for your choice. **(4)**
   ii) Should Colliers PLC charge a lower or higher price for the new bar than for a bar which is in Stage 3 of its product life cycle? Give reasons for your choice. **(4)**
   iii) Where should Colliers PLC advertise the new bar? Give reasons for your answer. **(4)**

2002

Dream Days Ltd is a travel firm which organises and sells special event trips and holidays such as shopping weekends in Paris and trips to major sporting events.

a) Is Dream Days Ltd a good name for the firm? Give reasons for your answer. **(2)**
b) The following is part of a questionnaire that Dream Days Ltd is planning to use to research the market for the kind of holiday it sells.

Dream Days Ltd – Market Research

1 What is your gender?   Male   [ ]   Female   [ ]

2 How much do you   Below £10,000   [ ]   £10,000–£20,000   [ ]
   earn each year?   £20,000–£30,000 [ ]   Above £30,000   [ ]

   i)   Explain why firms carry out this type of market research.   **(4)**
   ii) Write down **two** more questions Dream Days Ltd could ask in the market research
        questionnaire. Explain how these questions could be useful.   **(2)**
c) Dream Days Ltd sells a one-day trip from Bowton Airport to Monaco for people who want to
   watch the Formula 1 motor racing grand prix. The trip will cost customers £195. The price
   does not include the travel from the airport to the race. Dream Days Ltd needs to decide
   between two options:

   Option One: To charge the customers an extra £5 each for transport by coach from the airport
                to the race.
   Option Two: Leave the price as it is and let customers find their own way from the airport to
                the race either by public transport or by taxi.

   i)   State which of these options you would recommend. Give reasons for your answer.   **(6)**
   ii) If the cost to Dream Days Ltd is £150 for each customer and the trip is sold at £200
        per customer, calculate the mark-up. Show your working.   **(2)**

Business Behaviour – Production

SECTION 4

A*–B Questions

1998
What problems might result from the increased use of technology by a business? **(4)**

2002
Day Dreams Ltd sells a day trip to Monaco for the Formula 1 motor racing grand prix. The forecasts costs and revenues are shown below.

> **Dream Days Ltd – Trip to Monaco – Forecast of Cost and Revenues**
>
> - The variable costs of the trip are £50 per person.
> - The fixed costs of the trip are £30,000.
> - The price of a place on the trip is £200.
> - The maximum number of persons on the plane is 300.

i) State the number of places that Dream Days Ltd will need to sell to break even. You may use any method you are familiar with to produce an answer. **(6)**
ii) Calculate the profit that Dream Days Ltd would make if it sold 300 places on the trip. Show your working. **(3)**
iii) Explain why Dream Days Ltd should take care when using business forecasts such as break-even. **(4)**

Specimen Paper (2003 Exam)
John Taylor runs a garage which does car repairs and maintenance work and also fits car alarms. He fits the car alarms himself and employs a mechanic for the car repair and maintenance work.

Evaluate this division of labour in relation to the business. **(10)**

C–D Questions

1998
Carlton Press Ltd produce a range of educational books. They print the books themselves.

i) Which method of production – job, batch or flow – do you think would be most suitable for printing the books? Give reasons for your answer. **(4)**
ii) How might Carlton Press Ltd benefit from the increased use of technology in the printing process? **(4)**

John Taylor runs a business fitting car alarms. As part of his business plan, John prepared the following information about the revenue and the cost of fitting the car alarms:

- Selling price – £200
- Variable costs per alarm – £150

i) Use this information to complete the table below: (2)

Number of car alarms sold	Total Fixed Cost	Total Variable Cost	Total Cost	Total Revenue
10	1000	1500	2500	2000
20	1000	3000	4000	
30	1000		5500	6000
40	1000	6000	7000	8000

ii) Use the information in the table to complete a break-even chart. (6)

E–G Questions

1998
Carlton Press Ltd produce a range of educational books. They print the books themselves.
They intend to introduce new technology into the printing process.

Explain why the printers that Carlton Press Ltd employ may not want the introduction of the new technology. (6)

1999
David Morris owns a market stall, Jeans and Ts, selling jeans and T-shirts. The pie chart below shows the costs of selling a pair of jeans.

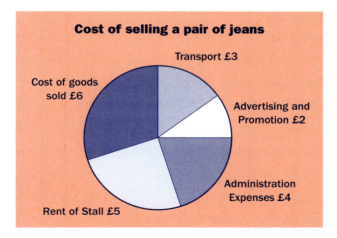

Cost of selling a pair of jeans

Transport £3

Cost of goods sold £6

Advertising and Promotion £2

Administration Expenses £4

Rent of Stall £5

i) How much does David pay for a pair of jeans? (1)
ii) What is the total cost of selling a pair of jeans? (1)
iii) What percentage of the total cost of a pair of jeans pays for the rent of the stall?
     Show your working. (3)

iv) State **two** administration expenses that David is likely to pay to run his business. **(2)**

v) From the pie chart, state **one** fixed cost and **one** variable cost. **(2)**

2000

The following table shows the costs and revenues of producing and selling boxes of chocolate at Colliers PLC.

Output: Number of Boxes Per Week	Total Cost of Production	Average Cost Per Box	Total Revenue (£1.50 Per Box)
10,000	£20,000	£2.00	£15,000
20,000	£30,000	£1.50	£30,000
50,000	£40,000	???	£75,000
100,000	£50,000	£0.50	£150,000

i) At which number of boxes of output does the firm
   - Break even?
   - Make a loss
   - Make most profit? **(3)**

ii) What is the average cost of producing 50,000 boxes? **(1)**

iii) The following are some costs that Colliers PLC must pay when producing chocolates:

   costs of ingredients   the electricity bill

   interest payments on a bank loan   overtime pay for production workers

   rent for the factory

State **two** costs that are fixed costs of production and **two** that are variable costs of production. **(4)**

Business Behaviour – Financial Information and Decision-making

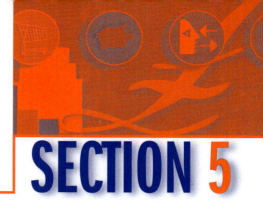

SECTION 5

A*–B Questions

1999

Carlton Press Ltd publishes educational books. The Trading and Profit and Loss Accounts for the years 1996 and 1997 are given below.

Carlton Press Ltd: Profit and Loss Accounts for years ending 31 December 1996/7		
	1996 (£s)	**1997 (£s)**
Sales	330,000	580,000
Cost of Sales	200,000	300,000
Gross Profit	130,000	280,000
Interest Payable	0	1000
Administration Expenses	100,000	240,000
Net Profit before Taxation	30,000	39,000
Taxation	8000	12,000
Profit after Tax	22,000	27,000
Dividends	2000	3000
Retained Profit	20,000	24,000

i) Why are dividend payments important to a business? **(2)**

ii) Would the shareholders of Carlton Press Ltd be pleased with the performance of the company in 1997 compared with the performance in 1996? Give reasons for your answer. **(7)**

2000

Colliers PLC manufactures and retails chocolates. The following table is a summary of the performance of Colliers PLC in 1998 and 1999.

	1998	1999	Change from 1998 – 1999
Turnover	£100	£120	20%
Net profit	£20	£30	
Dividends per share	10p	9p	–10%

a) Discuss the changes that may have caused the rise in turnover between 1998 and 1999. **(6)**

b) Calculate the percentage change in net profit from 1998 to 1999. Show your working. **(3)**

2001

Below is an extract from the balance sheet of TechWorld Ltd that was drawn up in February 2001.

TechWorld Ltd	
Extract from Balance Sheet at 1 February, 2001	
	£m
Current Assets	
Stock	6
Debtors	1
Cash at Bank	1
Current Liabilities	
Trade creditors	9
Taxation owed	1

Evaluate the position of TechWorld Ltd in the light of these figures. **(4)**

2002

Dream Days Ltd sells special event holidays. Tables 1 and 2 below show financial information for Dream Days Ltd.

Using the information in Tables 1 and 2 above, evaluate the performance of Dream Days Ltd in 2001 compared with 2000. **(9)**

Table 1: Profit and Loss Figures for Dream Days for the Financial Years Ending 31 December 2000 and 2001

Year	Profit
2000	£4m
2001	£5m

Table 2: Summary Balance Sheets for Dream Days Ltd as at 31 December 2000 and 2001

	2000		2001	
	£m	£m	£m	£m
Fixed Assets		10		12
Current Assets	20		27	
Current Liabilities	15		17	
Current Assets minus Current Liabilities		5		10
Net Assets		**15**		**22**
Capital and Reserves				
Share Capital		10		10
Long Term Liabilities		5		12
Capital Employed		**15**		**22**

2001

TechWorld Ltd sells computer software and hardware. The diagram below shows the pattern of sales that TechWorld Ltd achieved during 1999.

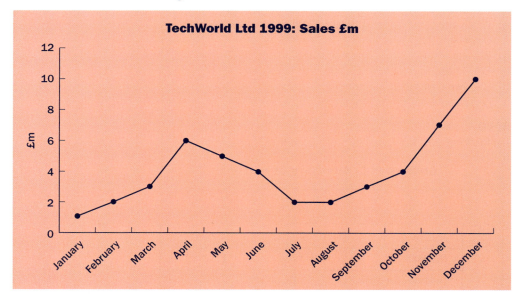

The total costs of production of TechWorld Ltd are spread evenly over the year and are at about £3m per month.

Explain, and illustrate, how this information could be used by TechWorld Ltd when planning its cash flow. **(4)**

2002

Dream Days Ltd sells special event holidays and trips. It uses forecasts as part of its business planning. Explain why Dream Days Ltd should take care when using business forecasts such as break-even forecasts. **(4)**

C–D Questions

No separate questions included for these grades.

E–G Questions

1998

The Trading and Profit and Loss Accounts for Carlton Press Ltd, a book publisher, are shown below.

Carlton Press Ltd: Profit and Loss Accounts for years ending 31 December 1996/7		
	1996 (£s)	**1997 (£s)**
Sales	330,000	580,000
Cost of Sales	200,000	300,000
Gross Profit		280,000
Expenses	100,000	240,000
Net Profit	30,000	

i) Calculate:
   The Gross Profit in 1996
   The Net Profit in 1997 **(2)**
ii) Give **two** examples of expenses that the business might pay. **(2)**
iii) Which **one** of the following taxes will Carlton Press Ltd pay on its profits: Income Tax, Corporation Tax, VAT. **(1)**
iv) Why are profits important for a business? **(3)**
v) Explain **two** ways in which Carlton Press Ltd may be able to increase its profits. **(4)**
vi) Give **two** reasons why the shareholders of Carlton Press Ltd would be pleased with the performance of the company in 1997 compared with 1996. **(2)**

2000

The following table is a summary of the performance of Colliers PLC in 1998 and 1999.

Colliers PLC: Summary of Performance 1998 and 1999

	1998	1999	Change from 1998–1999
Turnover	£100 m	£120 m	20%
Net profit	£20 m	£30 m	
Dividends per share	10p	9p	–10%

i) State what happened to sales income between 1998 and 1999. **(2)**
ii) Tick one of the boxes next to each statement to say if it may have been a likely cause of the change in sales that took place between 1998 and 1999.

Event	Likely Cause	Not a Likely Cause
Colliers PLC sold chocolates at higher prices in 1999 than they did in 1998		
Wage levels fell and unemployment rose during 1999		
Colliers PLC increased the amount that it spent on advertising in 1999 compared with 1998		

(3)

2001

TechWorld Ltd sells computer hardware and software. The diagram below shows the pattern of sales that TechWorld Ltd achieved during 1999.

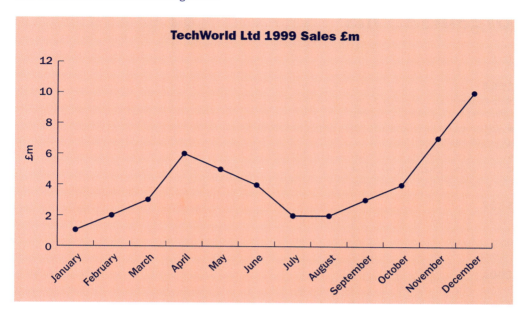

TechWorld Ltd 1999 Sales £m

i) In which month are sales
- at their lowest
- at their highest? **(2)**
ii) Suggest one reason for each of the following:
- High sales of computers in November and December
- Low sales of computers in July and August. **(2)**

People in Organisations

A*-B Questions

1994

Marpete Trailer Tents has agreed a no-strike deal with the trade union that represents workers that it employs. This agreement has the following features:

- Only one union will be able to negotiate pay and conditions on behalf of all workers.
- Labour can be used flexibly.
- Arbitration is binding on both management and the union.
- All employees have the same status.

Give reasons why both the employees and the management have accepted the deal. **(8)**

1997

Suzanne runs a bakery. She needs to recruit three new workers for the business.

Draw up a plan for recruiting and selecting workers who will suit her needs. Explain each of the stages in the process. **(12)**

2001

TechWorld Ltd is a chain of shops. It sells computer hardware and software including games. They received a large number of applications for sales assistant jobs that had been advertised.

i) Recommend **two** sources of information about the applicants that would have helped them to decide whom to employ. Give reasons for your answers. **(6)**

ii) All employees of TechWorld Ltd are given health and safety training. Explain why health and safety is important to firms like TechWorld Ltd. **(6)**

iii) Recommend **one** method of motivation that the TechWorld Ltd might use for the following workers. Give reasons for your answer.
   - The sales assistants.   • The sales manager of the firm. **(8)**

Specimen Paper (2003 Exam)

John Taylor runs a garage. He employs a mechanic who does repair and maintenance work on cars. As the manager of the business, John will need to motivate his mechanic to work well.

Recommend **one** method of motivating the mechanic involving pay and **one** method that does not involve pay that would be appropriate for John to use. Give reasons for your recommendations. **(8)**

C-D Questions

1998

Sunil Mandraker works as a salesperson for Carlton Press Ltd, a publisher. His payslip is shown here.

i) Complete the pay slip to show the value of Net Pay. **(1)**

ii) State **three** deductions that might be taken from Sunil's pay. **(3)**

iii) Why is commission an appropriate method of pay for Sunil? **(3)**

CARLTON PRESS LTD			
Date: 28 March, 1998 Employment No: 22548		Name: Sunil Mandraker National Insurance No: YW523784A	
Pay and Allowances		Deductions	
Salary	1100.00	Deduction 1	196.10
Commission	108.80	Deduction 2	84.62
		Deduction 3	113.48
Total Gross Pay	1208.80	Total Deductions	394.20
Net Pay			

1999

Wynne and Co Ltd manufactures clothes. Most of the employees are members of a trade union.
What benefits might they gain from this? **(4)**

2000

Colliers PLC manufactures and retails chocolates. It provides induction training for its new employees.

i) Describe the main features of an induction programme that would be suitable for workers who are new employees at Colliers PLC. **(3)**
ii) Colliers PLC is concerned about health and safety in the factory. Explain why health and safety matters are important to Colliers PLC. **(4)**
iii) Recommend **two** methods by which Colliers PLC may make their workers aware of health and safety matters in the factory. Give a reason for each choice. **(4)**

2002

Dream Days Ltd sells special event trip and holidays. It needs to recruit 20 cabin crew to serve people on its flights. Dream Days Ltd received 120 applications for the 20 jobs.

i) Recommend the methods of selection Dream Days Ltd should use to choose from the applicants. Give reasons for your recommendations. **(4)**
ii) Dream Days Ltd must train the new cabin crew about what to do in an emergency. Recommend whether Dream Days Ltd should use on-the-job or off-the-job training for this. Give reasons for your answer. **(4)**

E–G Questions

1999

Wynne and Co Ltd make clothes. It intends to employ more workers once the business expands. The job description below is for three extra clerical workers they need.

Job Description: Clerical Assistants

Department: Administration and Personnel

Main Tasks:
To assist with the creation and maintenance of computer records.
To type letters and minutes of meetings.
To act as receptionists on occasions.
To deal with telephone enquiries as appropriate.
To operate office machinery (photocopier, faxes, etc.) as required.
To keep records of stationery and materials used and order as required.

Responsible to: Office Manager

---

i) State **two** places that Wynne and Co Ltd should advertise the jobs. Give reasons for your answers. **(4)**
ii) State **two** skills that the workers will need to do the job well. Give reasons for your answer. **(4)**
iii) Describe the following methods of calculating pay:
  ● Piece rate
  ● Commission
  ● Profit-sharing scheme
  ● Hourly rate **(8)**
iv) Which of the above methods of paying workers would encourage the following employees of Wynne and Co Ltd to work hard? Give reasons for your answer.
  a) Machinists who sew T-shirts together
  b) Clerical Assistant
  c) Sales Representative **(3)**

2001

a) TechWorld Ltd has a chain of shops. It sells computer hardware and software, including computer games. The owners of the shops need to recruit sales assistants to work in the shops.

    i)   Recommend **four** skills or qualities that sales assistants would need in order to be successful. **(4)**

    ii)   Evaluate how useful each of the following sources of information about people would be in helping TechWorld Ltd when choosing whom to employ as sales staff.
- Interviews
- References
- Written tests **(6)**

    iii)   The newly appointed shop assistants would be given full training. Explain why TechWorld Ltd would give this training. **(6)**

b) The name of three methods of motivating workers are given in the box below, along with descriptions of different methods of motivation.

Name of Method	Description of Method
A) Fringe Benefits B) Piece Rates C) Profit Sharing	1) Workers will receive extra money if the firm performs well. 2) Workers are able to buy company products at reduced prices. 3) The worker is paid for each item that he or she produces.

    i)   Match the number of the correct description with the name of the method. **(3)**

    ii)   Recommend one method, other than those given in the question above, that TechWorld Ltd should use to motivate the sales assistants to work well. Give reasons for your answer. **(3)**

2002

Dream Days Ltd sells special event trip and holidays. It needs to recruit 20 cabin crew to serve people on its flights.

i)   State **four** skills or qualities that the cabin crew staff will need in order to do their jobs well. **(4)**

ii)   To advertise the cabin crew jobs, Day Dream Ltd designed the following advertisement:

AIR HOSTESSES WANTED

Dream Days Ltd

Apply to John Sanders

Recommend how you would improve the information in the advertisement. Give reasons for your recommendations. **(4)**

A*-B Questions

1995

During the period 1988 to 1992 many businesses in Moorshire had difficulties because of falling sales. Describe **two** ways in which a cut in interest rates could have helped businesses during this period. **(8)**

1999

Wynne and Co Ltd produce clothing. They intend to invest to expand their factory. Why do governments sometimes give grants to firms to help to finance this kind of investment? **(3)**

2002

State and explain two legal considerations that firms must take into account when promoting staff. **(4)**

C-D Questions

2000

Explain why the government has strict controls on advertising. **(2)**

2000

Colliers PLC manufacture chocolate. They are concerned about health and safety in the factory. Explain why health and safety matters are important to Colliers PLC. **(4)**

2001

The following headlines appeared in newspapers in 2000.

'Unemployment rises for third month'	**'Interest rates rise again'**

Explain why these events may have caused the sales of computers in the UK to fall in 2000. **(4)**

2002

The following headlines appeared in the newspapers in 2002. Dream Days Ltd sells special event holidays such as trips to Paris for shopping and trips to sporting events.

'Incomes continue to grow'	**'Government cuts tax on flights'**

Explain how each of these events may affect the sales of special event holidays. **(4)**

2002

State and explain **two** ways in which the government could encourage firms to use more information technology. **(6)**

Specimen Paper (2003 Exam)

State three things you would expect to be included in a contract of employment. **(3)**

E-G Questions

1999

The map on the following page shows the main business area of the town of Bowton. Look at the map and answer the questions that follow:

a) i)   Is it good for the businesses on the industrial estate to be near the railway station? Give reasons for your answer.
   ii) Is the bus station in a good location?

Main business areas in the town of Bowton

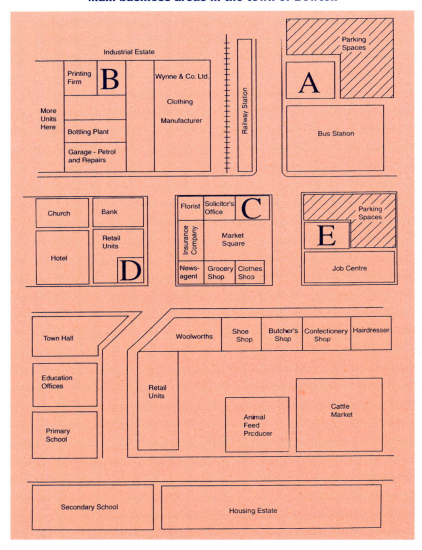

iii) The letters A–E show sites where there are buildings that are suitable for a shop or an office. Where do you think it would be good to locate the following businesses. Give reasons for your answer.
- A taxi rank
- A newsagent **(4)**

The following questions are relevant to Section 1: The External Environment of Business.

b) i) From the map, give **two** examples of manufacturing businesses. **(2)**

ii) From the map, give **two** examples of business that are in the tertiary sector of the economy. **(2)**

iii) Explain how the bank may help the owner of the grocery store. **(2)**

iv) Explain how the private businesses may help the people in the town. **(2)**

v) Expain how the local council may help the private businesses. **(2)**

vi) From the map, give **two** examples of businesses that are likely to be in the private sector of the economy. **(2)**

vii) From the map, give **two** examples of organisations that are likely to be in the public sector of the economy. **(2)**